# The Natural History Museum

## On the trail of
# Incredible
# Dinosaurs

William Lindsay

DK

DORLING KINDERSLEY
London • New York • Sydney

A DORLING KINDERSLEY BOOK

www.dk.com

**Project editor** Monica Byles
**Editor** Nicola Deschamps
**Art editors** Diane Thistlethwaite, Penny Lamprell, and Peter Radcliffe
**Managing art editor** Chris Scollen
**Managing editors** Dawn Sirett and Jane Yorke
**Production** Louise Barratt, Susannah Straughan, and Neil Palfreyman

**Research** Mary Ann Lynch
**Illustration** Simone Boni/L.R. Galante
**Dinosaur models** Graham High/Jeremy Hunt/Centaur Studios
**Model photography** Dave King
**Museum photography** Lynton Gardiner
**UK consultant** Dr Angela Milner, The Natural History Museum, London
**US Consultant** Dr Mark Norell, The American Museum
of Natural History, New York

Published in Great Britain by
Dorling Kindersley Limited,
9 Henrietta Street, London WC2E 8PS

4 6 8 10 9 7 5

# CONTENTS

# INTRODUCTION

About 230 million years ago an extraordinary group of animals appeared on Earth – dinosaurs. Dinosaurs were reptiles. They had scaly skins and laid eggs that had tough, waterproof shells. They lived only on land; there were no swimming or flying dinosaurs.

The earliest dinosaurs were quite small, two-legged meat-eaters, but they had something that gave them a distinct advantage over all the other reptiles – the ability to walk upright. Their legs were positioned directly beneath their bodies. This helped to support their body weight and balance the head and tail-ends. All other reptiles had legs that stuck out sideways. The dinosaurs' straight legs and balanced bodies meant that they could run fast, using just their back legs. This left their front limbs free for feeding and for attack or defence. Those dinosaurs that were really large could support their weight on all four legs and still move about easily. Scientists think that the main reason why dinosaurs became so successful was their ability to walk upright. These amazing creatures soon came to dominate life on land and remained supreme for more than 150 million years until their dramatic disappearance – an extinction that remains a mystery to this day. However, by studying the fossilized remains of dinosaurs, scientists have been able to piece together a great deal about the lives of these incredible animals.

This book takes you on a journey of discovery into the lost worlds of four great dinosaurs: *Tyrannosaurus rex*, *Barosaurus*, *Corythosaurus*, and *Triceratops*. You will find out how complete skeletons of these dinosaurs were found, excavated, and pieced together. Then you will discover how these creatures lived. Use the glossary and pronunciation guide on pages 92 and 93 to help you with unfamiliar words.

**THE NATURAL HISTORY MUSEUM** **Dr Angela Milner**
**Head of Vertebrates and Anthropology Division**
**The Natural History Museum, London**

NOTE: IN THIS BOOK WE HAVE SOMETIMES USED "*TYRANNOSAURUS REX*" (THE FULL, TWO-WORD SCIENTIFIC NAME FOR THIS DINOSAUR) BECAUSE IT IS WIDELY KNOWN. FOR THE OTHER THREE DINOSAURS WE HAVE USED THE FIRST PART OF THEIR NAMES ONLY. THEIR FULL SPECIES NAMES ARE AS FOLLOWS: THERE ARE TWO SPECIES OF *BAROSAURUS* — *BAROSAURUS LENTUS* AND *BAROSAURUS AFRICANUS*; *CORYTHOSAURUS*' FULL SCIENTIFIC NAME IS *CORYTHOSAURUS CASUARIUS*; *TRICERATOPS*' FULL SCIENTIFIC NAME IS *TRICERATOPS HORRIDUS*.

# TYRANNOSAURUS REX

*Tyrannosaurus rex* lived in western North America between 67 and 65 million years ago. It was one of the largest meat-eating animals that has ever lived on land, and one of the last dinosaurs to walk the Earth.

Fossil remains of *Tyrannosaurus rex* are rare. Apart from single teeth, fewer than twenty fossil specimens have been found, and only five or six of these are reasonably complete skeletons. One of the best finds of all, collected in 1908 by the famous American dinosaur hunter Barnum Brown, features in this book.

How do we know so much about *Tyrannosaurus rex* from so few remains? Careful study of its bones and teeth provides information about *Tyrannosaurus rex's* lifestyle and its place in evolution. We now know that it was not related to other large meat-eating dinosaurs but to advanced small meat-eaters like *Deinonychus* and *Troodon*, and that its closest living relatives are the birds. We also know what other kinds of dinosaurs shared its world.

However, the remains of *Tyrannosaurus rex* will never reveal what the living animal was really like. Palaeontologists can only make educated guesses as to how it behaved, how fast it ran, and the colour of its skin. Facts such as these remain a mystery, lost forever in the past.

# TYRANT LIZARD

*T*yrannosaurus rex is one of the most famous of all the dinosaurs. Even its name makes you imagine huge, nightmarish monsters. But *Tyrannosaurus* was no make-believe monster. Millions of years after its death, scientists are now able to piece together this great creature from its fossilized remains, providing some answers to many puzzling questions.

**Scaly skin**
Rare impressions of dinosaur skin have been found fossilized in ancient rocks. It was thick, tough, scaly, and waterproof, similar to that of modern-day reptiles, like the crocodile.

*Tyrannosaurus rex*
(Tie-ran-oh-saw-rus recks) means "king of the tyrant lizard".
*Tyrannosaurus* means "tyrant lizard".

**Two types of dinosaur**
Dinosaurs are divided into two groups by the shape and position of their hip or pelvic bones. "Bird-hipped" or ornithischian dinosaurs were plant-eaters; their two lower hip bones pointed backwards and down to accommodate their large guts. "Lizard-hipped" or saurischian dinosaurs, such as *Tyrannosaurus rex,* were primarily meat-eaters and had shorter, less bulky guts, allowing their hip bones to sit closer together. One of their two lower hip bones pointed forwards and their other bone pointed backwards.

*Heterodontosaurus*
"bird-hipped" dinosaur

*Struthiomimus*
"lizard-hipped" dinosaur

**Walking tall**
Unlike most reptiles, whose legs sprawl out at the sides of their bodies, dinosaurs stood on legs held straight beneath their bodies. This enabled dinosaurs to move about more easily than other reptiles. Some dinosaurs walked on four legs. Others, such as *Tyrannosaurus rex,* walked on two.

## Meat-eater

Carnivores, or meat-eaters, such as *Tyrannosaurus rex* had sharp teeth and claws for slicing into flesh. *Tyrannosaurus rex* had extremely strong jaws that were powered by mighty muscles, enabling it to open its mouth so wide that it could have swallowed a human in just two bites!

## FACT FILE

- **Lived:** 67–65 million years ago, during the late Cretaceous Period

- **Family:** Tyrannosaurids, one of the coelurosaurian group

- **Dinosaur type:** Lizard-hipped (saurischian)

- **Maximum life span:** Possibly up to 100 years

- **Diet:** Meat of dinosaurs and other animals

- **Weight when alive:** Up to 7 tonnes (little over 6 tons)

- **Height:** 6 m (18 ft)

- **Length:** 14 m (42 ft)

- **Top speed:** Possibly up to 25 km/h (15 mph)

Like most two-legged predators, *Tyrannosaurus rex* could move quickly. However, *Tyrannosaurus* could probably not run at speed for long distances because of its great size

## Lost worlds

Dinosaur species appeared and died out over three periods of the Earth's history. *Tyrannosaurus* lived at the end of the Cretaceous Period.

**TRIASSIC PERIOD**
248–205 million years ago

**JURASSIC PERIOD**
205–145 million years ago

**CRETACEOUS PERIOD**
145–65 million years ago

# FOSSIL FINDS

The story of the death, fossilization, and discovery of one *Tyrannosaurus rex* spans more than 65 million years. When *Tyrannosaurus* died at the end of the Cretaceous Period, it was buried under sand and mud, where its skeleton was slowly transformed into fossil.

In July 1908, Barnum Brown, one of America's greatest dinosaur hunters, spotted the exposed *Tyrannosaurus* fossil bones jutting out of rocks near Hell Creek, Montana, USA. Eight years earlier, Brown had discovered the unfamiliar remains of a new dinosaur, later named *Tyrannosaurus rex*. But this second find was much more complete. Indeed, this particular dinosaur is still used to identify new *Tyrannosaurus* fossil specimens today.

**Journey through the earth**
After its death around 65 million years ago, the body of this *Tyrannosaurus rex* was not destroyed by other animals. The skeleton survived intact in its rocky grave for millions of years, until earth movements and weathering exposed it once more.

**Dry season**
A long drought has dried up the lush swamps and forests. A few plants still grow along old river-beds.

**Wet season**
Later in the year, heavy rains bring flash floods. Dead animals and plants are buried in sand and mud as the waters subside.

**New life**
Hundreds of years later, the river has changed course. Other dinosaurs now feed on the plants that grow by the river.

**1 Alive and well**
The fearsome *Tyrannosaurus* prowls along drying river-beds, where other dinosaurs gather to feed and drink.

**2 Washed away**
Killed by disease, attack, or drowned, *Tyrannosaurus* is carried off in floodwaters.

**3 Dead and buried**
Buried under sand and mud, only bones and teeth remain. The dinosaur's soft flesh has long since rotted away.

**Terrible tooth**
Dinosaur teeth are often well preserved as fossils, because they are hard and resistant to decay. A *Tyrannosaurus* tooth may be as long as 18 cm (7 in) with a sharp, serrated edge for cutting and tearing the flesh of its prey.

**4 Turned to stone**
The skeleton is now buried under many layers of rock. Chemicals have slowly changed the bones into hard fossils.

**5 Inside the Earth**
Movements deep below the Earth's crust force the *Tyrannosaurus* skeleton closer towards the surface. The fossil bones are now cracked and broken.

**In the footsteps of Barnum Brown**
The rocks of Hell Creek, Montana, USA, were formed in the Late Cretaceous Period of the Earth's history, during the time of the last dinosaurs. Today, the rocks are scoured for treasures by fossil hunters.

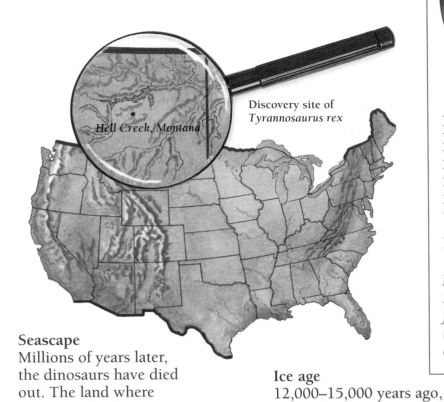

Hell Creek, Montana

Discovery site of *Tyrannosaurus rex*

## DINOSAUR DETECTIVE
### *Barnum Brown (1873 – 1963)*

Barnum Brown joined the American Museum of Natural History (AMNH), New York, in 1897. Nicknamed "Mr Bones", Brown worked at the museum for 45 years. His skill in discovering fossils helped to give the AMNH one of the finest dinosaur collections in the world.

1873  *Born at Carbondale, Kansas, USA.*
1895  *Discovered a **Triceratops** skull in Wyoming, USA.*
1897  *Joined AMNH as a palaeontologist at age of 24.*
1900  *Discovered the first fossils of **Tyrannosaurus rex**.*
1908  *Found the second **Tyrannosaurus rex** specimen.*
1934  *Made his greatest discovery of over 20 dinosaur skeletons at Howe Quarry, Wyoming.*
1963  *Died one week before his 90th birthday in New York.*

**Dinosaur diggers**
*Barnum Brown (centre, front row) with his field team on one of many dinosaur field trips.*

**Seascape**
Millions of years later, the dinosaurs have died out. The land where they once lived is now covered by sea.

**Ice age**
12,000–15,000 years ago, the sea has gone and the land is now frozen. Earth movements have pushed up mountains.

**6 Into daylight**
The rock of the ancient river-bed has been carved by wind and rain into hills and canyons. Weathering has finally brought the *Tyrannosaurus* fossils back to the surface of the Earth.

# DIGGING FOR DINOSAURS

Like many dinosaur discoveries, the *Tyrannosaurus rex* specimen of 1908 was found in desolate, open country, far from the nearest settlement. Barnum Brown and his field team set up camp in the badlands of Montana, five days' travel by horse-drawn wagon from the nearest railway.

The excavation took three months of backbreaking work. Some of the *Tyrannosaurus* bones were easily removed from sand but others were buried in rock as hard as granite. Scrapers, picks, shovels, and even dynamite were used to dig free the fossil bones.

**Plaster jacket containing fossil**

**Materials needed to make a plaster jacket**

**Chisels for chipping rock**

**Sacking**

## 1 Excavating the fossils
Once rubble had been cleared from around the skeleton, the fossil hunters began to chip rock away from individual bones. When the fossils were exposed, they were strengthened with glue, covered with tissue paper, and wrapped in sacking soaked in plaster of Paris.

## 2 Shipping the fossils
Once the protective plaster jacket had dried, each fossil could be removed from site. The fossils were hoisted into wooden crates. Each heavy crate was hauled by horse and cart to the railway, some 240 km (150 miles) away from the excavation site.

**Missing or fragile bones, like those of the skull, were modelled in plaster**

## 3 Studying the fossils
At the Museum in New York, the plaster jackets were removed and the delicate fossils carefully restored. The bones were then compared with those of other *Tyrannosaurus* finds. At last, the complete dinosaur skeleton could be carefully pieced together.

**4 Skeleton display**
In 1915, the scientists began to prepare the original fossils for a new museum display. Ropes and pulleys held all the heavy bones in place while the mount was built.

Trowel for mixing plaster

A lighter plaster cast was hung in place of the fragile and heavy skull

Ropes held all the bones securely in position, while the supporting metal framework was built around the fossil skeleton

The dinosaur builders worked from wooden platforms, laid across scaffolding, high above the Museum floor-level

**Mini-dinosaurs**
The dinosaur builders made detailed scale models, one-sixth of life size, showing every bone in the skeleton of *Tyrannosaurus rex*. These models helped the scientists to experiment with different display positions for their full-size mount. The model shown here demonstrates how *Tyrannosaurus rex* might have been mounted, gnawing on a carcase.

# MONSTER IN MOTION

Tyrannosaurus rex was a ferocious hunter of its fellow dinosaurs and other animals. It had a massive head and a stout neck that could deliver a crushing and deadly blow to its prey. Tyrannosaurus used its strong toes and sharp claws to hold down its victims, while its savage, razor-sharp teeth sliced into their flesh. Few animals could escape a Tyrannosaurus on the attack.

**Speeding dinosaur**
Some scientists believe that a charging Tyrannosaurus could reach a top speed of over 25 km/h (15 mph). Other experts claim it was capable of running at up to 65 km/h (40 mph), as fast as a white rhino.

**3 Spotting prey**
Tyrannosaurus sights a young dinosaur, grazing apart from its herd. Tyrannosaurus turns its head for a better view.

**2 On the prowl**
Tyrannosaurus moves forward, swinging powerful legs under its huge body.

Tyrannosaurus rex had strong legs tucked under its bulky body, which supported its 7 tonne (6 ton) weight

**8 Deadly bite**
The knife-sharp fangs of Tyrannosaurus rex close in on its next meal. One swift bite slices through the windpipe and blood vessels in the neck, and crushes bone.

**1 Hungry hunter**
A hungry Tyrannosaurus hunts for a likely victim. Its keen senses are ready to detect the presence of another predator that might steal its kill.

As it moved along, *Tyrannosaurus* used its long tail to counterbalance the weight of its massive body

**5 On the attack**
Now in full attack, *Tyrannosaurus* charges forward towards its prey.

**4 Ready to strike**
Sweeping its muscular tail around, *Tyrannosaurus* moves in for the kill. If its strike is unsuccessful, *Tyrannosaurus* will have wasted vital energy and alerted the herd of grazing dinosaurs to danger.

**7 In for the kill**
*Tyrannosaurus* lunges forward with open jaws to catch its prey.

**6 Towering tyrant**
*Tyrannosaurus* throws up its head and roars. Rearing overhead, *Tyrannosaurus* is a terrifying sight to its victim.

# GIANT JAWS

*Tyrannosaurus rex* had one of the biggest and strongest heads of all the dinosaurs. This ferocious meat-eater could kill its prey with one crushing bite from its giant sabre-toothed jaws, while a twist of its powerful neck tore away the first mouthful of meat. Even the large plant-eating dinosaurs of the time that were shielded with tough, bony plates would have been savaged by *Tyrannosaurus'* immensely strong jaws and dagger-like fangs. Like other meat-eating dinosaurs, *Tyrannosaurus* was able to grow new teeth to replace those that were broken or worn down.

### Skull discovery

The *Tyrannosaurus* skull shown here, found by Barnum Brown at Hell Creek, Montana, in 1908, is more than 1 m (over 3 ft) long. The enormous skull and jaw bones were big enough to swallow smaller dinosaurs whole.

A front view of the skull shows the huge bones, slightly crushed by fossilization

Openings for the air passages to the nostril

Scientists have left some of the rock between the bones to support the shape of the heavy skull

Giant, serrated teeth curve backwards, designed to grip and rip apart carcases. The teeth form a deep cutting edge as they increase in size from the front to the middle of the jaws

New teeth grew to replace those that were old and worn

Fine holes along the margin of the jaws show where blood vessels passed out of the bone to the skin

Strong lower jaw had a large area of bone where the jaw muscles were attached

### Bone-crusher

*Tyrannosaurus rex* had enormous and powerful jaws, operated by thick masses of muscle. Other dinosaurs could make their mouths larger by flexing their skull bones at special joints, just as some reptiles do today.

Small bony crest on the roof of the skull

Eye socket

Muscles from the stout neck were connected to the wide area of bone at the back of the skull

Spaces between the skull bones made the head lighter and left room for the muscles

**Powerful neck**
*Tyrannosaurus* needed extra strong neck muscles to support and move its mighty skull. *Tyrannosaurus* could move its head in all directions, which helped it to hold down struggling prey.

*Tyrannosaurus rex* may have had eyes positioned for better sight when hunting than other dinosaurs. Eyes that faced forward may have helped it focus on prey as it charged in for the kill

Slit-like ear opening led to the hearing organ inside the skull

Large tongue helped process its food before swallowing

# KILLER INSTINCT

*Tyrannosaurus rex* was an animal well adapted for hunting. Bigger than any of the other meat-eating dinosaurs of its time, a 8 tonne (7 ton) *Tyrannosaurus* was powerful enough to attack even a 6 tonne (6 ton) heavily armoured *Triceratops*. Its giant size was matched by an enormous appetite, and *Tyrannosaurus* seized every opportunity for catching a passing meal – the bigger the kill, the less hunting it had to do.

*Tyrannosaurus* was equipped with excellent tools for hunting and killing. In addition to the dinosaur's great size, strength, and fearsome teeth, it probably had good senses for seeing, hearing, and smelling its prey.

**Staying alive**
Like all animals, *Tyrannosaurus rex* had to eat to live. Although it may have stolen kills made by smaller carnivores, *Tyrannosaurus* was better equipped than most to hunt its own prey.

Some worn *Tyrannosaurus rex* teeth show where the dinosaur would have bitten through soft flesh to the hard bone

**1 Finding a meal**
*Tyrannosaurus rex* has killed its prey and must devour it quickly before it is stolen by other carnivores.

*Tyrannosaurus rex* may have needed to eat its own weight in meat every week

**2 Tearing flesh**
*Tyrannosaurus* holds down the carcase with its clawed feet and rips off lumps of meat with its jaws. The dinosaur swallows its meal in large chunks without chewing.

**Focusing on prey**
Many dinosaurs had eyes at the sides of their head and saw a different view from each eye. Some animals, such as humans, have eyes that face forwards and can form a single view. This lets them judge distances accurately. *Tyrannosaurus rex* may have had eyes that faced forwards, helping it to spot prey. No one knows if *Tyrannosaurus rex* saw in tones of grey or in colour.

Single view from forward-facing eyes in colour and in black and white

Double view from sideways-facing eyes in colour and in black and white

Bird-like feet pinned the carcase to the ground

Teeth were curved and serrated, designed to slice huge chunks of meat from the carcase

**3 Facing the competition**
A second hungry *Tyrannosaurus* approaches, desperate to share in the kill. *Tyrannosaurus* prepares to defend its meal, and roars in an effort to frighten away its rival.

# FEROCIOUS FIGHTER

Tyrannosaurus rex was the top predator living in North America in the Late Cretaceous Period. Like lions today, Tyrannosaurus preyed on the plant-eating animals in its area. But unlike lions, which hunt in packs, Tyrannosaurus rex probably hunted alone.

Skeletons of large carnivores like Tyrannosaurus rex are usually found singly, not in groups. In one part of Canada, only 5 out of 100 dinosaur finds have been large meat-eaters. Tyrannosaurus may have needed to eat a lot of dinosaur meat to satisfy its huge appetite.

**Face to face**
Although most animals will try to avoid a fight, they may attack one another over food. Few dinosaurs would have risked attacking Tyrannosaurus rex. However, one damaged Tyrannosaurus skull has been found that suggests that a second Tyrannosaurus might have attacked, perhaps to steal a kill.

A face-to-face struggle between two hungry Tyrannosaurus would have been one of the most fearsome battles ever

**Gaping jaws**
The tooth-lined jaws of Tyrannosaurus rex are its main weapons. The gaping mouth and fierce roars of the bigger animal may scare the other off without a fight.

**Deadly dance**
Tyrannosaurus challenges its rival, shifting to and fro, to show off its strength and size. This display may force the rival away.

**Ready to charge**
The massive, muscular legs are ready to carry Tyrannosaurus in a headlong charge at its enemy, if it finally has to fight for its meal.

**Cretaceous hunting-ground**
*Tyrannosaurus* would have preyed on many species of dinosaur. Most would have kept away from this ferocious predator.

**Safety in numbers**
*Triceratops*, one of the most common dinosaurs of the period, browse in herds for protection.

*Saurolophus*

*Edmontosaurus*

*Ornithomimus*

*Parasaurolophus*

*Ankylosaurus*

**Fast runners**
Duck-billed dinosaurs, like *Saurolophus*, *Edmontosaurus,* and *Parasaurolophus*, as well as the fast-running *Ornithomimus*, feed nervously as the fight continues. At the first sign of danger, they will escape into the safety of the forest.

**Armoured defence**
An armoured *Ankylosaurus* backs off from the battle. Even with its powerfully muscled tail club, the animal prefers to avoid any danger.

**Safe in the river**
River turtles have picked clean the carcase of a dead dinosaur. Swept there by last season's floodwaters, the skeleton is now left half-buried in the silted shallows of the stream.

**Swinging tails**
Tails raised for balance, the two dinosaurs shift position and try to catch one another off guard.

# TYRANNOSAURUS SPECIMEN AND FAMILY FACTS

- **Specimen number:** AMNH 5027
- **Excavated by:** Barnum Brown
- **Excavation:** 1908, at Hell Creek, Montana, USA
- **Bones found:** Almost complete skeleton – missing the forelimbs and some leg bones, which were modelled in plaster

- **Where displayed:** American Museum of Natural History (AMNH), New York, USA*
- **First constructed:** 1915 – made up primarily from original fossil bones. Ropes and pulleys used during construction to hold all heavy bones in place

 ON THE MUSEUM TRAIL

### A museum guide to tyrannosaur specimens

#### EUROPE

**France**
(*Tarbosaurus*, *Tyrannosaurus*) National Museum of Natural History, Paris
**Germany**
(*Tyrannosaurus*) Senckenberg Nature Museum, Frankfurt am Main
(*Tyrannosaurus*) Geological and Palaeontological Museum, Münster
(*Tyrannosaurus*) Institute and Museum for Geology and Palaeontology, University of Tübingen, Tübingen
**Spain**
(*Tyrannosaurus*) Natural Science Museum, Madrid

Sweden
(*Tyrannosaurus*) Palaeontological Museum, Uppsala University, Uppsala
**United Kingdom**
(*Tyrannosaurus*) Birmingham Museum, Birmingham
(*Tyrannosaurus*, *Albertosaurus*, *Daspletosaurus*) The Natural History Museum, London

**Dinosaur display**
This is the specimen found by Brown in 1908. It was the first *Tyrannosaurus* skeleton ever built. It towered over other dinosaurs in the halls of the AMNH for many years.

#### USA

(*Tyrannosaurus*) University of Michigan Exhibit Museum, Ann Arbor, Michigan
(*Tyrannosaurus*) University of California, Museum of Paleontology, Berkeley, California
(*Albertosaurus*, *Tyrannosaurus*) American Museum of Natural History, New York City, New York
(*Tyrannosaurus*) Carnegie Museum of Natural History, Pittsburgh, Pennsylvania
(*Albertosaurus*, *Tyrannosaurus*) National Museum of Natural History, Smithsonian Institution, Washington, D.C.

*Tyrannosaurus rex* lived about 65 million years ago, at the end of the Cretaceous Period. It was one of the last dinosaurs

*AMNH 5027 was completely remounted in a new pose for the revised AMNH dinosaur gallery opened in 1996.

24

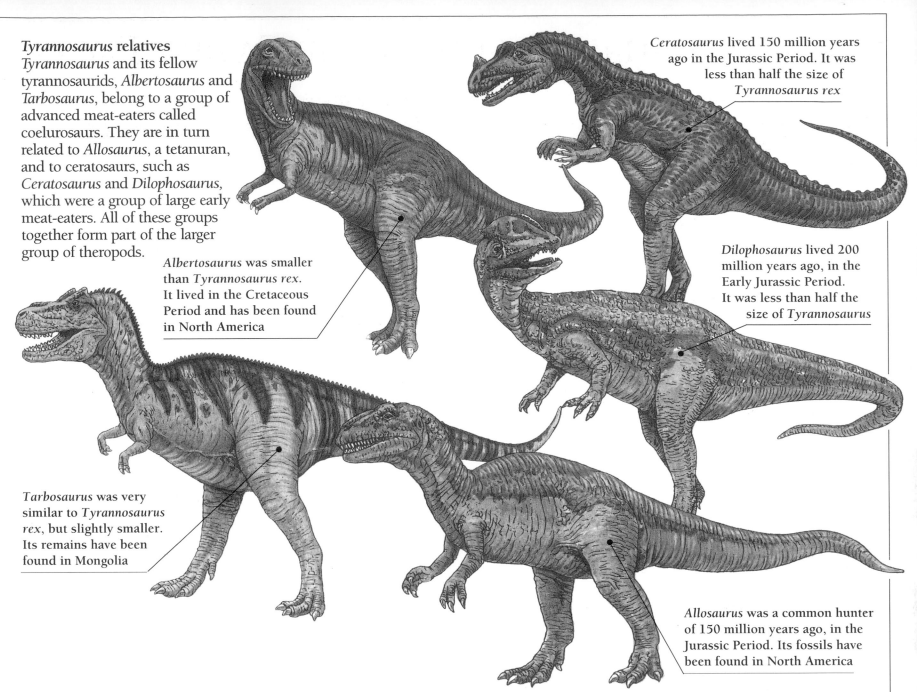

**Tyrannosaurus relatives**
*Tyrannosaurus* and its fellow tyrannosaurids, *Albertosaurus* and *Tarbosaurus*, belong to a group of advanced meat-eaters called coelurosaurs. They are in turn related to *Allosaurus*, a tetanuran, and to ceratosaurs, such as *Ceratosaurus* and *Dilophosaurus*, which were a group of large early meat-eaters. All of these groups together form part of the larger group of theropods.

*Albertosaurus* was smaller than *Tyrannosaurus rex*. It lived in the Cretaceous Period and has been found in North America

*Ceratosaurus* lived 150 million years ago in the Jurassic Period. It was less than half the size of *Tyrannosaurus rex*

*Dilophosaurus* lived 200 million years ago, in the Early Jurassic Period. It was less than half the size of *Tyrannosaurus*

*Tarbosaurus* was very similar to *Tyrannosaurus rex*, but slightly smaller. Its remains have been found in Mongolia

*Allosaurus* was a common hunter of 150 million years ago, in the Jurassic Period. Its fossils have been found in North America

**Worlds apart**
Dinosaur remains have been found on every continent. New species of dinosaurs evolved and adapted over millions of years as climates and landscapes changed. This map shows areas where *Tyrannosaurus* and other theropods have been found.

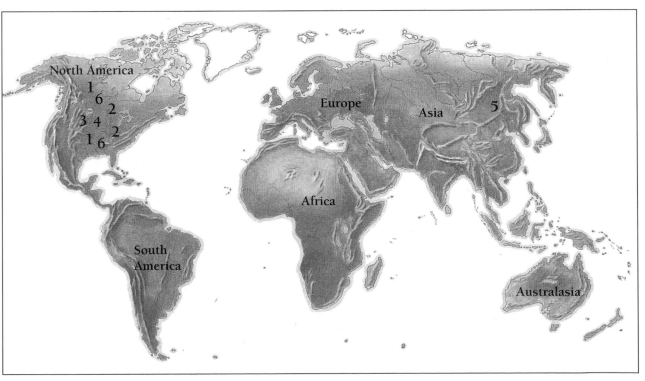

**Key to map**

1  *Albertosaurus*
2  *Allosaurus*
3  *Ceratosaurus*
4  *Dilophosaurus*
5  *Tarbosaurus*
6  *Tyrannosaurus*

# BAROSAURUS

*Barosaurus* was one of the largest animals that has ever lived on land. This enormous creature, together with similar long-necked, four-footed dinosaurs, was the top plant-eater of its day, around 150 to 140 million years ago.

It is difficult for us today to imagine these gigantic animals wandering across the landscape. *Barosaurus* and its relatives were many times larger than the biggest land animal living today, the African elephant. But, like the African elephant, *Barosaurus* was a social animal and probably lived in herds or family groups. Footprints and trackways of *Barosaurus* and its relatives provide us with vital clues to the everyday lives of these dinosaurs. We can see from 150-million-year-old trails left along a muddy river bank in North America that a herd of these magnificent animals walked along with the young animals following in the adults' footsteps.

The *Barosaurus* you will read about in this book is displayed at the American Museum of Natural History in New York. It has been mounted rearing up on its hind legs to protect its baby from an attacking *Allosaurus*. Would *Barosaurus* really have been able to do this? Judging from the strongly constructed bones in its legs and the base of its tail, this is quite possible. But no one knows for sure. It is the job of palaeontologists to make accurate guesses, based on the study of the dinosaur's remains.

# HEAVY LIZARD

*B*arosaurus was one of the tallest of the dinosaurs. Standing on all four legs, it could reach treetops as high as a three-storey building. Standing up on its back legs it could reach as high as a five-storey building! Its long neck was held up by very strong, but lightweight, bones. And because of its length, scientists think it might have had special valves in its blood vessels to make sure enough blood reached its brain. *Barosaurus* skeletons have been found in North America and Africa, but no complete skull has yet been discovered.

*Barosaurus*
(barrow-saw-rus)
means "heavy lizard"

## Little and large
Dinosaurs came in all shapes and sizes; they were not all giants like *Barosaurus*. Some dinosaurs were as small as the modern-day chicken, while some, such as *Struthiomimus*, were the size of a horse, and others, such as *Heterodontosaurus*, were the size of a dog.

*Barosaurus* had a neck 9 m (30 ft) long – even longer than the necks of *Diplodocus* and *Apatosaurus*, its close relatives. With such a long neck, plant-eating *Barosaurus* could feed some distance from where it stood

*Struthiomimus*
"lizard-hipped" dinosaur

## Lizard-hipped
*Barosaurus* was a "lizard-hipped" or saurischian dinosaur. One of the two lower bones of its pelvis pointed forwards, and the other pointed backwards.

*Barosaurus* walked on four legs, which were positioned directly beneath its body

## Dinosaurs through the ages

*Barosaurus* lived in the Jurassic Period, long before *Tyrannosaurus rex,* which lived at the end of the Cretaceous Period.

**TRIASSIC PERIOD**
248–205 million years ago

**JURASSIC PERIOD**
205–145 million years ago

**CRETACEOUS PERIOD**
145–65 million years ago

### Prehistoric feeder

*Barosaurus* was a plant-eater, or herbivore, belonging to a group of dinosaurs called the sauropods. *Barosaurus* had a huge barrel-shaped body, designed to hold the large amounts of food it ate every day.

### FACT FILE

- **Lived:** 150 million years ago, Jurassic Period
- **Family:** Diplodocids, part of sauropod group
- **Dinosaur type:** Lizard-hipped (saurischian)
- **Maximum life span:** Perhaps 100 years
- **Diet:** Rough plant material
- **Weight when alive:** About 25 tonnes (25 tons)
- **Height:** Over 15 m (50 ft), from ground to head-level
- **Length:** 24 m (80 ft)
- **Top speed:** About 7 km/h (more than 4 mph)

*Barosaurus* had a whip-like tail, which it may have used to frighten off attackers

### Heavy weight

*Barosaurus* weighed more than eight elephants. It had sturdy, pillar-like legs, which ended in elephant-like feet with five toes. Its back legs were even bigger than its front legs.

# FOSSIL TREASURES

One of the world's richest hoards of dinosaur fossil treasure was discovered among stony, barren hills in Utah, USA. A wide river flowed here in the Jurassic Period, where dinosaurs gathered to eat and drink. Over many years, dinosaur remains were buried under mud and sand and were slowly transformed into fossils.

In 1908, Earl Douglass, an American fossil collector, first came to investigate the site for the Carnegie Museum of Natural History. Four years later, he found an almost complete skeleton of *Barosaurus*. Douglass' discoveries were so important that in 1915 the dinosaur graveyard was made a national monument.

**1 Fit and feeding**
*Barosaurus* feeds on ferns and horsetails on the bank of a broad river.

**2 Death bed**
Killed by disease, attack, or drowned, the body of *Barosaurus* has been washed by floodwaters on to a sandbank in the river.

**3 Buried underground**
Thousands of years later, most of the skeleton of *Barosaurus* lies buried under sand, mud, and gravel. Only bones remain. The dinosaur's soft flesh has long since rotted away.

**Journey through time**
*Barosaurus* died in the Late Jurassic Period. Its fossilized skeleton was preserved deep in the Earth for 150 million years until its discovery in 1912.

## DINOSAUR DETECTIVE
### *Earl Douglass (1862 – 1931)*

Earl Douglass was a skilled hunter of dinosaur fossils. In 1908, he discovered the important fossil site, later named Dinosaur National Monument. For 16 years he worked to establish the Monument as a unique working museum.

| | |
|---|---|
| 1862 | *Born at Medford, Minnesota, USA.* |
| 1902 | *Joined the staff of the Carnegie Museum, Pittsburgh, Pennsylvania, USA.* |
| 1909 | *Found and began to excavate Apatosaurus.* |
| 1909/24 | *Excavated Apatosaurus, Stegosaurus, Allosaurus, Diplodocus, Camarasaurus, Barosaurus, and Camptosaurus.* |
| 1912/14 | *Excavated skeleton of Barosaurus.* |
| 1914 | *Completed mount of Apatosaurus at the Carnegie Museum.* |
| 1924 | *Left the Dinosaur National Monument.* |
| 1931 | *Died at Salt Lake City, Utah, USA, aged 69.* |

**Fossil hunter**
*Earl Douglass, standing next to a partly excavated Diplodocus skeleton in 1922.*

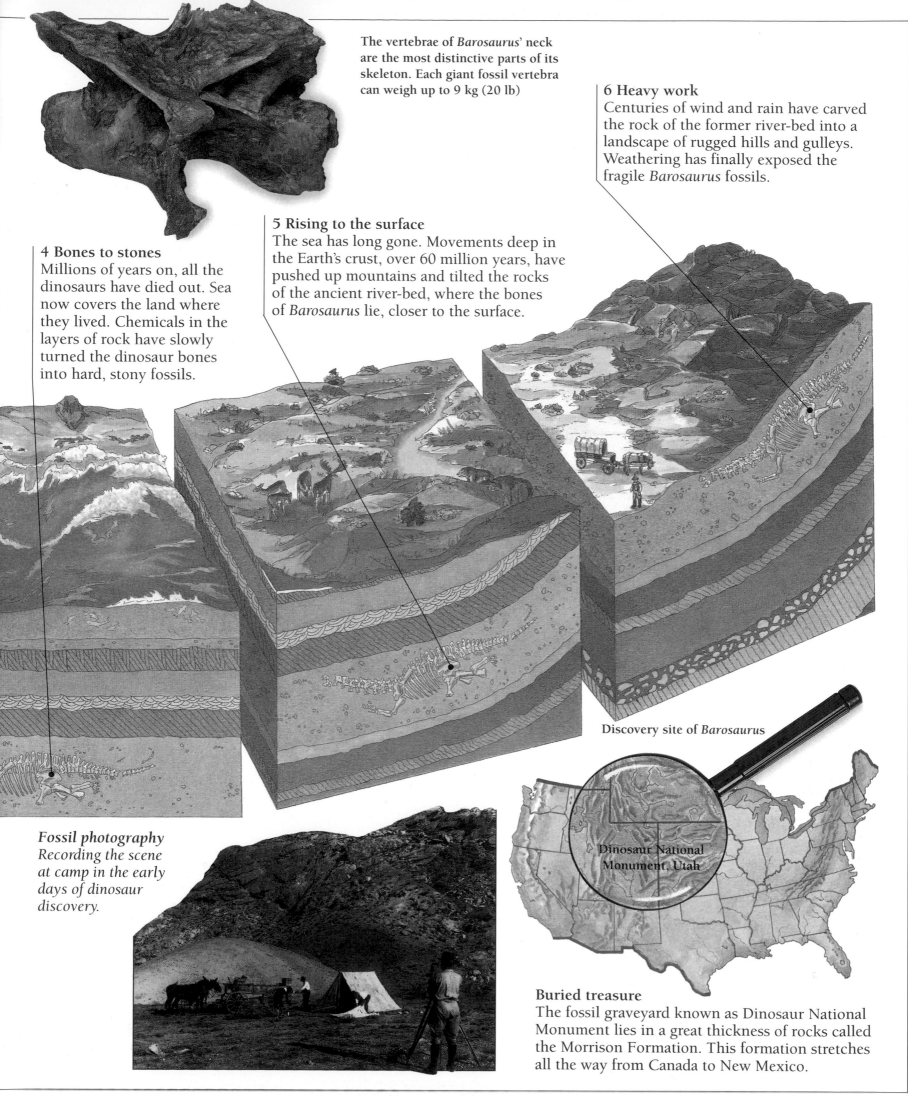

The vertebrae of *Barosaurus*' neck are the most distinctive parts of its skeleton. Each giant fossil vertebra can weigh up to 9 kg (20 lb)

## 6 Heavy work
Centuries of wind and rain have carved the rock of the former river-bed into a landscape of rugged hills and gulleys. Weathering has finally exposed the fragile *Barosaurus* fossils.

## 5 Rising to the surface
The sea has long gone. Movements deep in the Earth's crust, over 60 million years, have pushed up mountains and tilted the rocks of the ancient river-bed, where the bones of *Barosaurus* lie, closer to the surface.

## 4 Bones to stones
Millions of years on, all the dinosaurs have died out. Sea now covers the land where they lived. Chemicals in the layers of rock have slowly turned the dinosaur bones into hard, stony fossils.

Discovery site of *Barosaurus*

*Fossil photography*
*Recording the scene at camp in the early days of dinosaur discovery.*

Dinosaur National Monument, Utah

**Buried treasure**
The fossil graveyard known as Dinosaur National Monument lies in a great thickness of rocks called the Morrison Formation. This formation stretches all the way from Canada to New Mexico.

# DINOSAUR JIGSAW

Earl Douglass and his dinosaur diggers took two years to excavate *Barosaurus* on behalf of the Carnegie Museum in Pittsburgh, Pennsylvania. The Museum, however, traded sections of the skeleton with two other museums as spare parts to help complete their own sauropod specimens. The fossil bones might still be separated, were it not for the dinosaur hunter Barnum Brown. He succeeded in reuniting the *Barosaurus* skeleton at the American Museum of Natural History in New York.

Cracks in the ancient fossil bones were repaired with glue and plaster

**Digging for dinosaurs**
Douglass and his men used shovels, hammers, picks, chisels, and even dynamite to dig the fossil skeleton of *Barosaurus* from its rocky grave.

**Controlled explosion**
Dynamite was needed to blast away some of the hardest rock. This was formed from the mud and sand of the ancient river-bed, now turned to solid stone.

**Grid system**
The fossil bones were excavated from a steep quarry face. A grid was painted on to the rock to make it easier to record where each bone was found.

Neck vertebra, slightly crushed during fossilization

Rounded end of bone fitted snugly into hollow of the next vertebra

**Plaster jackets**
Once exposed, the fragile bones were wrapped in a protective jacket of plaster and sacking. When the plaster was dry, the heavy bones were hauled up the steep rockface.

**Slow sledge**
Mules dragged the bones, in their plaster jackets, out of the quarry by sledge. Many journeys were needed to remove all the fossil bones.

**Waste tip**
Tonnes of rock were chipped from the rockface during the excavation. Waste rubble was pushed in carts along a short railway and then tipped down the steep slope of the hillside.

Back vertebra, about 61 cm (24 in) long

## Fossil trading
Barnum Brown, of the American Museum of Natural History in New York, had reunited all the parts of the *Barosaurus* skeleton by 1929.

## American Museum of Natural History, New York
This museum exchanged money and fossils in return for the complete fossil skeleton of *Barosaurus*.

## Carnegie Museum, Pittsburgh, Pennsylvania
This museum had received part of *Barosaurus'* tail from the University of Utah.

## Smithsonian Institution, Washington, D.C.
The Smithsonian owned bones from the neck and body of *Barosaurus* and part of a limb.

## University of Utah Salt Lake City, Utah
The university museum received $5,000 and a fossil horse skeleton in exchange for *Barosaurus* remains.

## Dinosaur National Monument, Utah
The original site of excavation of *Barosaurus*. Its fossils were later split up between three different museums.

## Basement storage
The *Barosaurus* fossil bones were stored in the basement of the American Museum of Natural History. Sixty years later, the Museum finally decided to prepare the fossils for display.

Bones were stored on open shelves in the Museum's basement

All pieces of fossil from the skeleton were kept together

These shelves were filled with *Barosaurus* vertebrae

## DINOSAUR DETECTIVE

### Barnum Brown (1873 – 1963)

Barnum Brown was a great dinosaur hunter and collector. In his years at the American Museum of Natural History in New York, he filled the dinosaur halls with many of the fossil skeletons he had excavated. Although he did not discover *Barosaurus* himself, he knew that this was an important specimen to acquire for the Museum's dinosaur collection.

1873   *Born at Carbondale, Kansas, USA.*
1897   *Joined the staff of the American Museum of Natural History (AMNH) in New York.*
1900   *Discovered the world's first known specimen of **Tyrannosaurus rex**.*
1908   *Discovered a second, more complete, specimen of **Tyrannosaurus rex**.*
1910   *Began collecting dinosaur remains along the Red Deer River, Alberta, Canada.*
1912   *Discovered the skeletons of the duck-billed dinosaur, **Corythosaurus**, and the horned dinosaur, **Centrosaurus**.*
1916   *Completed dinosaur hunting along the Red Deer River.*
1929   *Gathered together the separated parts of the **Barosaurus** skeleton at the AMNH.*
1934   *Excavated the remains of over 20 sauropod dinosaurs at Howe Quarry, Wyoming, USA.*
1942   *Retired from the AMNH.*
1963   *Died, aged 89, in New York.*

# DINOSAUR DOUBLE

The skeleton of *Barosaurus* was finally taken out of storage 80 years after its discovery. Museum scientists planned to put the bones on display. They wanted to mount the skeleton rearing up on its back legs, defending its young against an attacking *Allosaurus*. As the fossil bones were fragile and too heavy to display in this way, the scientists decided to make a lightweight plastic replica of the skeleton. Once the fossils had been restored and any missing bones modelled from special clay, casting could begin.

**Materials used to cast the fossilized bones**

Liquid plastic

Liquid rubber

Brushes

Cleaning fluid for brushes

### 1 Building dams
First, "dams" made of cardboard are used to divide the surface of each fossil bone, or group of bones. The dams stand like walls on the surface of the bone, and split it into sections. More dams are needed if the bone shape is complicated. The dams give flat edges to the moulds, so that all the parts of a replica bone will fit together neatly.

### 2 Making a rubber mould
Each part of the fossil bone and dam is now painted with layers of liquid rubber. When the rubber sets, it forms a perfect, flexible mould of the original bone's surface. The rubber mould is then peeled away from the fossil.

### 3 Supporting the mould
The rubber mould is strengthened with cotton gauze. A plastic jacket is made to support the outside.

## 4 Casting the bones
Next, the inside of the rubber mould is coated with liquid plastic. The plastic will copy every detail that has been moulded from the fossil's surface.

## 5 Assembling the cast
Sheets of glass fibre are added to the plastic to make light but strong casts of the fossil. The cast sections are then joined together to recreate the entire bone's shape.

## 6 Filling the cast
The hollow bone cast is made even stronger by pouring in a special liquid foam plastic. This foam sets hard to form a tough honeycomb centre.

## 7 Removing the mould
When the foam plastic has set hard inside the cast, the rubber mould and its supporting jacket are peeled away from the outside. At last, the perfectly shaped plastic copy of the original fossil bone is revealed.

## 8 Finishing touches
Finally, the rough edges left by the joins between the separate mould sections are carefully filed away. The plastic bone is then painted to match the colours of the original fossil.

## 9 Measuring up
The replica fossils are measured against a chart of the whole skeleton. Each plastic bone is then matched up against its neighbours to check the fit. Only when all the bones are complete – more than 200 – will the lightweight *Barosaurus* skeleton be ready for assembly in the museum.

# BUILDING BAROSAURUS

The *Barosaurus* skeleton was transported by road from Canada, where it was made, to New York for assembly at the American Museum of Natural History. Here, the task of assembling the *Barosaurus* mount in its unique rearing pose required expert construction skills. Specialists from many different fields – artists and model-makers, palaeontologists and engineers – all came together to reconstruct a dramatic scene that may have taken place around 150 million years ago.

A few of the many dinosaur builders whose varied skills helped to assemble the rearing *Barosaurus* mount

**1 The skeleton arrives**
Huge trucks deliver the replica *Barosaurus* bones safely to the Museum.

**2 Checking the plans**
Inside the Museum, detailed plans are consulted at each stage of the dinosaur's assembly. Even a small mistake in the positioning of body sections would be difficult to put right, once building is complete.

**3 Dinosaur ribcage**
The giant ribcage is unloaded in one piece. The ribs show the barrel shape of *Barosaurus'* vast body.

**4 Neck section**
The massive neck section is gently carried out from its trailer. The giant vertebrae are already threaded on to a supporting steel pipe.

**5 Rocky base**
A natural landscape is pieced together to make a realistic base for the *Barosaurus* mount. Latex rubber was painted on to rocky ground in Montana. When set, the rubber was peeled away and used as a mould to make a glass-fibre cast, or "land-peel".

**6 "Land-peel" scene**
The "land-peel" is assembled before building begins. It will help to recreate the scene of 150 million years ago.

**7 Lifting platform**
The hind legs and upper pelvis of *Barosaurus* are raised into the air using a lifting platform. The platform allows the dinosaur builders to lower the heavy legs gently on to the metal framework below.

**8 Tail piece**
Before the legs are finally put in place, the tail sections are moved into position. The supporting metal frame is then fixed together.

**10 Filling in the gaps**
Shielded from the hot, flying sparks by his helmet, a welder works quickly to join the steel frame running through *Barosaurus'* tail sections. A vertebra is then placed over each welded joint.

**9 Welding the framework**
The skeleton of the young *Barosaurus* is assembled in the foreground, as the steel rods of the mother's tail are welded together.

# HIGH-RISE SKELETON

The most dramatic stage in the reconstruction of *Barosaurus* was the joining of the long neck section to the rest of the skeleton. The rearing replica was designed to reach over 15 m (50 ft) into the air, and so the dinosaur builders needed a good head for heights!

Engineers used lifting platforms to work high above the skeleton

Great care was taken not to knock the fragile skeleton

Guide ropes helped to steady the neck section during the lifting process

**3 Danger from above**
Dwarfed by the huge structure, the builders line up the connecting rods by hand. The steel tubes that run through the neck and ribcage sections must fit together exactly to provide a strong support for the replica bones. A poorly constructed skeleton of this size would be in danger of collapsing.

**1 Hoisting the neck**
The long neck section is hoisted gently into the air with the help of two sturdy lifting platforms. From the ground, helpers use ropes to hold the neck steady and guide it over to the rest of the replica skeleton.

**2 Delicate operation**
The lightweight neck section is carefully lowered into position over the upright ribcage. At floor-level, team helpers look on anxiously.

Every section, including the neck vertebrae, is filled with lightweight foam plastic

**4 Safely in place**
At last, workers on the lower-level lifting platform signal that the neck and head section is slotted firmly into place.

During welding, the replica fossil bones were protected with fireproof cloth

**5 Finishing touches**
The steel supports of the neck are welded together. Care is taken to shield the bones from hot sparks, which could set them alight. Another stage in this daring reconstruction is complete.

# ATTACK AND DEFENCE

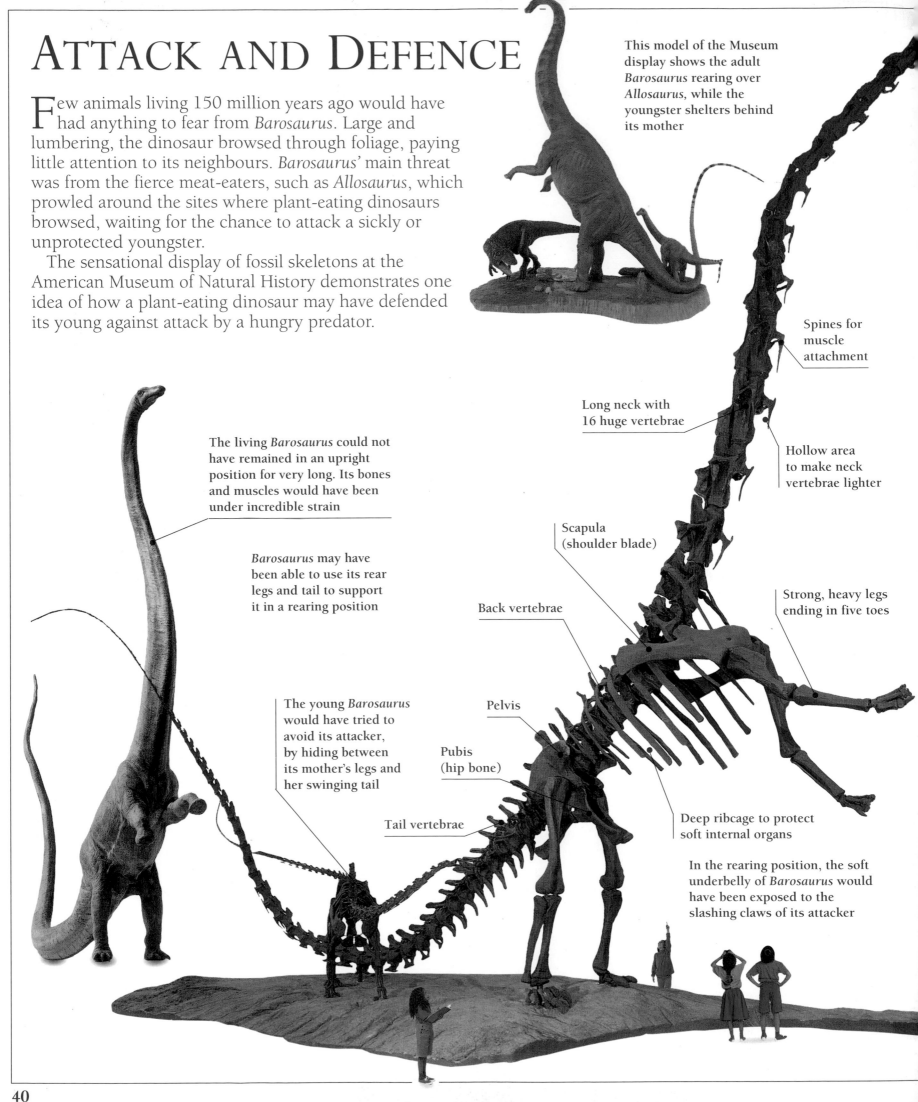

**F**ew animals living 150 million years ago would have had anything to fear from *Barosaurus*. Large and lumbering, the dinosaur browsed through foliage, paying little attention to its neighbours. *Barosaurus'* main threat was from the fierce meat-eaters, such as *Allosaurus*, which prowled around the sites where plant-eating dinosaurs browsed, waiting for the chance to attack a sickly or unprotected youngster.

The sensational display of fossil skeletons at the American Museum of Natural History demonstrates one idea of how a plant-eating dinosaur may have defended its young against attack by a hungry predator.

This model of the Museum display shows the adult *Barosaurus* rearing over *Allosaurus*, while the youngster shelters behind its mother

Spines for muscle attachment

Long neck with 16 huge vertebrae

Hollow area to make neck vertebrae lighter

The living *Barosaurus* could not have remained in an upright position for very long. Its bones and muscles would have been under incredible strain

Scapula (shoulder blade)

*Barosaurus* may have been able to use its rear legs and tail to support it in a rearing position

Back vertebrae

Strong, heavy legs ending in five toes

The young *Barosaurus* would have tried to avoid its attacker, by hiding between its mother's legs and her swinging tail

Pelvis

Pubis (hip bone)

Deep ribcage to protect soft internal organs

Tail vertebrae

In the rearing position, the soft underbelly of *Barosaurus* would have been exposed to the slashing claws of its attacker

The head of *Barosaurus* was modelled on that of *Diplodocus*, its close relative. A few *Barosaurus* skull bones have been found, but only in Africa. A complete skull has never been discovered

**Agile runner**
The replica skeleton of *Allosaurus* is mounted in a running position, with its tail outstretched for balance.

**1 Base framework**
The body and tail are fitted on to the legs and pelvis, which are mounted on a metal framework.

*Allosaurus* had small, powerful front limbs. Each hand had three sharp claws

*Allosaurus* stood upright like a bird, on three long toes

**2 Arms in place**
The bones of the shoulders, arms, and the dangerous claws are welded into place.

**Hungry hunter**
150 million years ago, *Allosaurus* was the chief predator among the dinosaurs of the land that is now North America. *Allosaurus* was 11 m (36 ft) long and weighed 1.8 tonnes (1.5 tons). It posed a deadly threat to a young *Barosaurus*.

Tail held high for balance

**3 Skull and bones**
The skull of *Allosaurus*, four times longer than a human head, is placed at the end of the smoothly curved neck. The replica skeleton is now complete.

Large, powerful legs for running at prey

The natural landscape base helps to set the scene of the Jurassic Period

# ON THE MOVE

*B*arosaurus lived at a time when the climate was warm with wet and dry seasons. Thick layers of mudstones, river sands, and gravels found in the ancient rocks at the Dinosaur National Monument show there were periods of heavy rains and flooding. Fossilized mud cracks indicate there were times of drought. For *Barosaurus* there was only one thing to do when the seasons changed – move on. Just as antelopes and zebra migrate over the African plains today, so the plant-eating dinosaurs of the Jurassic Period would have left behind the dead and drying plants in search of fresh feeding grounds.

**Steps in time**
Scientists have unearthed fossilized dinosaur footprints, left in soft sand and mud, which suggest how quickly the animals moved. Prints made by *Barosaurus* itself have not been identified, but other sauropod footprints suggest they may have walked at speeds of about 7 km/h (over 4 mph).

**High-rise defence**
Some scientists believe that sauropod dinosaurs like *Barosaurus* could rear up on their hind legs in defence against an attacker. Their tails may have been used as leverage and for support.

Sets of fossil dinosaur footprints suggest that many sauropods travelled together in herds

Although few *Barosaurus* skeletons have been found, it may also have travelled in herds

The absence of trails left by tails among dinosaur footprints indicates that sauropods walked with their tails held up off the ground

Patterns of dinosaur footprints have recently been found that suggest that young dinosaurs walked behind the adults when travelling in a herd

**Long-distance link**
Remains of *Barosaurus* have been found in Tanzania in Africa, as well as in South Dakota and Wyoming in North America. This fossil evidence shows that the continents of Africa and North America must have formed one land mass during the Middle Jurassic Period.

# GREEDY GIANT

*Barosaurus* was a giant plant-eater living during the Jurassic Period. The warm, wet climate meant that plenty of plants grew to satisfy this dinosaur's monster appetite. Although there were no grasses, *Barosaurus* and the other herbivores fed on ferns, horsetails, ginkgos, conifers, and many other plants that still grow today.

*Diplodocus*

**Gentle grazers**
Many dinosaurs grazed with *Barosaurus* on the lush floodplain or along the winding river.

*Barosaurus* needed to eat huge amounts of plant food every day to fuel its gigantic body

**Stony stomach**
*Barosaurus* rakes in plant matter with its peg-like teeth and then swallows it whole. Once in its stomach, the food is ground into a thick paste by hard, shiny pebbles called gastroliths.

*Barosaurus* swallowed stones to grind up its food, just as some birds do today

**Treetop browser**
The long neck of *Barosaurus* is useful for feeding on leaves high in the treetops. Instead of browsing at such a dizzy height, however, it may prefer to strip leaves from the lower branches.

**Whiplash tail**
*Barosaurus* stays on constant alert because of a prowling *Allosaurus*. If the *Allosaurus* threatens to attack its young, *Barosaurus* will lash out with its long tail to keep the predator at bay.

*Apatosaurus*

*Camptosaurus*

*Stegosaurus*

**Fast movers**
Small *Dryosaurus* lived in groups. They relied on speed to escape from danger.

**Ferocious hunter**
*Allosaurus* was a fierce carnivore that hunted plant-eaters.

**Riverside feeders**
Groups of *Apatosaurus* and single *Camptosaurus* browsed by the riverside.

**Hungry herbivores**
Both *Stegosaurus* with its bony plates, and large herds of the long-necked *Diplodocus*, grazed together on the plains.

The long neck of *Barosaurus* allowed its head to move in all directions, as the animal watched for danger

If a baby *Barosaurus* survived disease and attack, and found enough to eat, it might live to be 100 years old

**Baby food**
The young *Barosaurus* stays close to its parent, feeding on low-growing leaves and on ground plants such as ferns.

# BAROSAURUS SPECIMEN AND FAMILY FACTS

- **Specimen number:** AMNH 6341
- **Excavated by:** Earl Douglass
- **Excavation:** 1912–1914, at Dinosaur National Monument, Utah, USA
- **Bones found:** Four-fifths of skeleton, but no complete skull. Skull modelled on *Diplodocus*, its close relative
- **Where displayed:** American Museum of Natural History (AMNH), New York, USA
- **Year when constructed:** 1991; lightweight replica bones modelled in plastic and metal and used in place of original and valuable heavy fossils

---

## 🏛 ON THE MUSEUM TRAIL 🏛

### A museum guide to sauropod specimens

<u>EUROPE</u>

**France**
(*Diplodocus*) National Museum of Natural History, Paris
**Germany**
(*Brachiosaurus*) Humboldt University, Natural History Museum, Berlin
(*Diplodocus*) Senckenberg Nature Museum, Frankfurt am Main
(*Diplodocus*) Bavarian Institute for Palaeontology and Historical Geology, Munich
(*Diplodocus*) Institute and Museum for Geology and Palaeontology, University of Tübingen, Tübingen
**Italy**
(*Diplodocus*) G. Capellini Museum, Bologna
**Spain**
(*Diplodocus*) Natural Science Museum, Madrid

**United Kingdom**
(*Cetiosaurus*) Leicestershire Museum, Leicester
(*Camarasaurus*, *Diplodocus*) The Natural History Museum, London
(*Cetiosaurus*) University Museum, Oxford

**Unique display**
The AMNH in New York has the only *Barosaurus* skeleton on display in the world. A replica made of plastic and metal, the dinosaur rears up in the air, protecting its young from an attacking *Allosaurus*.

<u>USA</u>

(*Apatosaurus*, *Diplodocus*) Dinosaur National Monument, Jensen, Utah
(*Apatosaurus*, *Barosaurus*) American Museum of Natural History, New York
(*Apatosaurus*) Peabody Museum of Natural History, Yale University, Connecticut
(*Apatosaurus*, *Diplodocus*) Carnegie Museum of Natural History, Pittsburgh, Pennsylvania
(*Diplodocus*) National Museum of Natural History, Smithsonian Institution, Washington, D.C.

*Barosaurus* had a neck 9 m (30 ft) long. This animal lived around 150 million years ago, during the Jurassic Period

## Dinosaur world

The sauropod dinosaurs were the largest animals ever to live on land. Their fossils have been discovered on all the continents except Antarctica. This map shows where some members of the sauropod family have been found.

North America

Asia

Europe

Africa

South America

Australasia

### Key to map

1 *Apatosaurus*
2 *Barosaurus*
3 *Brachiosaurus*
4 *Camarasaurus*
5 *Diplodocus*
6 *Mamenchisaurus*

## Family trees

*Barosaurus* belongs to the diplodocid family, like *Apatosaurus* and *Diplodocus*. *Mamenchisaurus* was a close relative but *Brachiosaurus* and *Camarasaurus* were only distant cousins. All of them belong to a larger group of dinosaurs called the sauropods.

*Mamenchisaurus* had the longest neck known of all the dinosaurs. It lived at about the same time as *Barosaurus*, during the Late Jurassic Period

*Brachiosaurus* was taller than most dinosaurs. It also lived in the Late Jurassic Period

*Apatosaurus* was shorter than *Barosaurus* and lived at the same time and in the same area

*Diplodocus* was one of the longest dinosaurs. It also lived with *Barosaurus* in what is now North America

*Camarasaurus* was a bulky sauropod that lived alongside *Barosaurus*

The remains of *Barosaurus* have been found in North America and in Africa. A few skull bones have been discovered in Africa, but no complete *Barosaurus* skull has ever been found.

47

# CORYTHOSAURUS

*Corythosaurus* lived around 78 million years ago in western North America. It belonged to a large group of plant-eating dinosaurs called hadrosaurs, or duck-billed dinosaurs. Hadrosaurs were social animals that lived in herds. They can be divided into two groups: dinosaurs with spectacular head crests like *Corythosaurus* and flat-headed dinosaurs without crests.

By studying the helmet-shaped crest on the skull of *Corythosaurus*, scientists can gather clues about the dinosaur's lifestyle. Exciting research in the last few years has looked at hadrosaur fossils in the light of what we know about today's animals that live in herds. Members of a hadrosaur herd could recognize each other by their head crest shape, and they could probably distinguish between sexes in this way, too. The crests were hollow and enabled *Corythosaurus* to make loud trumpeting noises so that large herds could keep in touch with each other by sound as well as sight.

However, there is much that we still do not know about *Corythosaurus*. For instance, how many years did a newly hatched baby take to grow up? How long did one of these dinosaurs live? These are questions that we cannot yet answer. However, scientific methods of the future, as well as new fossil finds, may provide the answers and reveal more about these fascinating animals from the past.

# HELMET LIZARD

*Corythosaurus* was a crested member of the duck-billed family of plant-eating dinosaurs. It lived around 78 to 74 million years ago, near the end of the dinosaurs' reign. The crest on top of a *Corythosaurus'* head grew from hatching and varied in size. Enough fossils have been discovered for scientists to distinguish differences between the crests of male and female adults, and also between adults and babies. It is thought that an adult male's crest was larger than the female's and roughly the size and shape of half a dinner plate.

### Duck-billed dinosaurs
*Corythosaurus* was a member of the hadrosaur family of dinosaurs. Hadrosaurs are nicknamed "duck-bills" because of their broad, duck-like beaks. Some hadrosaurs grew up to 15 m long (49 ft), although *Corythosaurus* itself reached only 7.5 m long (almost 24 ft).

### Dinosaur skin colour
No one knows what colour the markings on dinosaur skin may have been. Some dinosaurs may have been coloured for camouflage, while others may have been brightly patterned to warn off predators. The markings shown here are one interpretation of how *Corythosaurus* may have looked.

*Corythosaurus* (korrith-oh-saw-rus) means "helmet lizard" after the hollow, bony, helmet-like crest on the dinosaur's head.

A curved, flexible neck helped *Corythosaurus* to turn its head to feed among tree branches

*Corythosaurus* could run upright on two legs or drop down on all fours

The tail of the *Corythosaurus* was not very flexible. It could probably move only a little from side to side. The tail was held up off the ground behind the body and helped *Corythosaurus* to keep its balance when walking on two legs

## FACT FILE

- **Lived:** Between 78–74 million years ago, during the Cretaceous Period
- **Family:** Hadrosaurids, the duck-billed dinosaurs
- **Dinosaur type:** Bird-hipped (ornithischian)
- **Diet:** Plant material, such as leaves, fruit, and seeds
- **Weight when alive:** About 4 tonnes (over 4 tons)
- **Height:** Approximately 3 m (10 ft)
- **Length:** Approximately 7.5 m (24 ft)
- **Top speed:** Possibly up to 32 km/h (more than 20 mph)

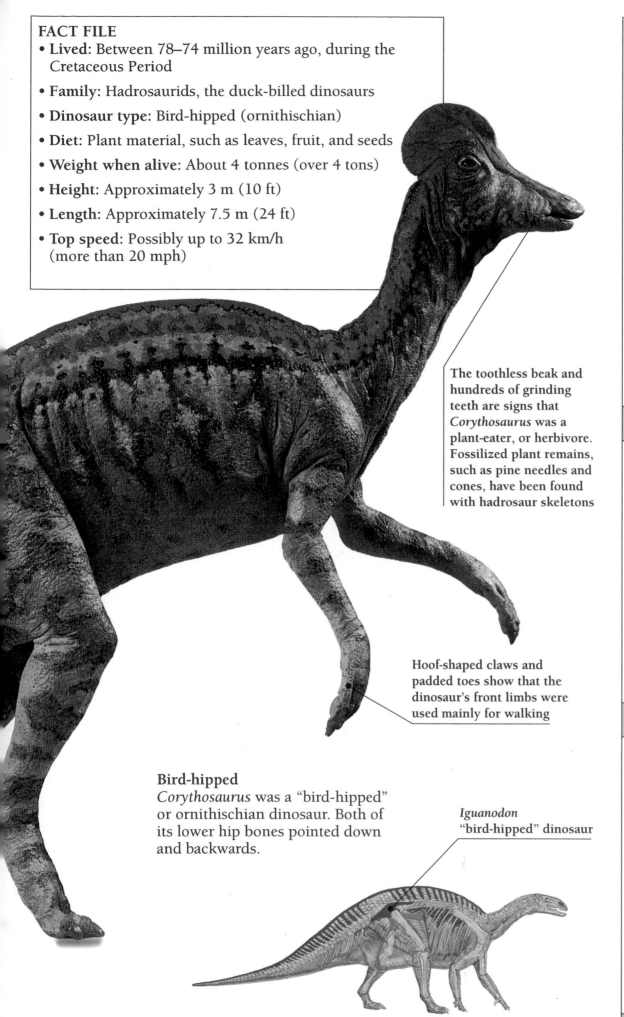

The toothless beak and hundreds of grinding teeth are signs that *Corythosaurus* was a plant-eater, or herbivore. Fossilized plant remains, such as pine needles and cones, have been found with hadrosaur skeletons

Hoof-shaped claws and padded toes show that the dinosaur's front limbs were used mainly for walking

**Bird-hipped**
*Corythosaurus* was a "bird-hipped" or ornithischian dinosaur. Both of its lower hip bones pointed down and backwards.

*Iguanodon* "bird-hipped" dinosaur

**Dinosaur times**
*Corythosaurus* lived towards the end of the Earth's Cretaceous Period, before *Tyrannosaurus rex*, but long after *Barosaurus*, which lived in the Jurassic Period.

**TRIASSIC PERIOD**
248–205 million years ago

**JURASSIC PERIOD**
205–145 million years ago

**CRETACEOUS PERIOD**
145–65 million years ago

# DINOSAUR DISCOVERY

In 1914, the famous dinosaur hunter, Barnum Brown, made a sensational find. He noticed fossil bones weathering out of rocks along the Red Deer River, near Steveville, Alberta, Canada. The bones were part of a beautifully preserved *Corythosaurus* skeleton – only the end of the tail and parts of the hands were missing.

Two years earlier, Brown had unearthed the first known specimen of *Corythosaurus*, but this second find was more complete. The bones were partly crushed, but they were still lying in their original positions, as if *Corythosaurus* had carefully lain down to die in soft, sandy mud, about 78 million years before.

**Bones to stones**
When animals and plants are buried underground, they are sometimes changed into hard replicas of themselves, called fossils. This change may take place over millions of years as chemicals in rocks and soil seep into the buried object.

**1 Food and drink**
About 78 million years ago, *Corythosaurus* pauses by a winding stream on a wide, flat plain. It feasts on the conifers, ferns, and flowers that grow there.

**2 Muddy waters**
A few years later, *Corythosaurus* lies dead on the bank of a river. The rains falling in the distant mountains will soon flood the river, sweeping mud and sand over the animal carcase.

**3 Buried dinosaur**
Over hundreds of years, the rivers move back and forwards across the plain, building up layers of mud and sand over the buried skeleton. Other dinosaurs now live above ground.

Tibia (shin bone)

***Corythosaurus* fossil**
Only the hard parts of the *Corythosaurus* skeleton, such as the bones and teeth, were fossilized. The softer flesh and skin were not preserved, but rotted away in the damp soil soon after the dinosaur's death.

Over millions of years, *Corythosaurus'* bones are buried deeper and deeper underground

# DINOSAUR DETECTIVE

## Barnum Brown (1873 – 1963)

Barnum Brown was one of the world's greatest dinosaur hunters. He found his first dinosaur fossil, a *Triceratops* skull, in 1895 and went on to fill the American Museum of Natural History (AMNH), New York, with many finds.

**1873** Born at Carbondale, Kansas, USA.

**1897** Joined AMNH as a palaeontologist, aged 24.

**1900** Discovered the first known remains of **Tyrannosaurus rex**.

**1910** Set off by boat to hunt dinosaurs along the Red Deer River, Alberta, Canada.

**1912** Discovered the first **Corythosaurus** near Steveville, Alberta.

**1914** Discovered a more complete specimen of **Corythosaurus**.

**1963** Died in New York, at the age of 89.

*Barnum Brown (to the right) on his flatboat on the Red Deer River*

## Dinosaur Provincial Park

Over 350 fossil skeletons, including that of *Corythosaurus*, have been found near the Red Deer River in Alberta, Canada. So many have been discovered that the area has been set aside as a dinosaur park.

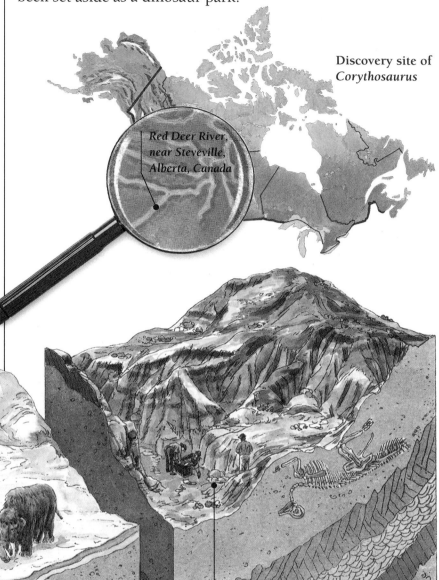

Discovery site of *Corythosaurus*

*Red Deer River, near Steveville, Alberta, Canada*

## 4 Death of the dinosaurs

65 million years ago, the dinosaurs have become extinct. The skeleton slowly turns to fossil as chemicals pass from the rocks into the bones.

## 5 Cold world

15,000 years ago, an ice age has spread over much of North America. Huge earth movements have pushed the rocks and the fossilized bones closer to the surface.

## 6 Exposed bones

Thousands of years of wind and rain have carved the rocks of the ancient river-bed into hills and gulleys. A few bones of the fossilized *Corythosaurus* have weathered out of the steep side of a canyon.

# FRAGILE FIND

In 1909, Barnum Brown visited a ranch near the Red Deer River, in Alberta, Canada. The ranch owner had found fossils high up in the barren canyons near his home. Brown identified the fossils as dinosaur bones and mounted an expedition on behalf of his employer, the American Museum of Natural History in New York.

Between 1910 and 1915, Barnum Brown and his team of dinosaur hunters used a flatboat, or barge, to travel down the river, stepping ashore to look for fossils in the nearby cliffs. In the summer of 1914, Brown and his colleagues excavated their best find, the well-preserved skeleton of an adult *Corythosaurus*.

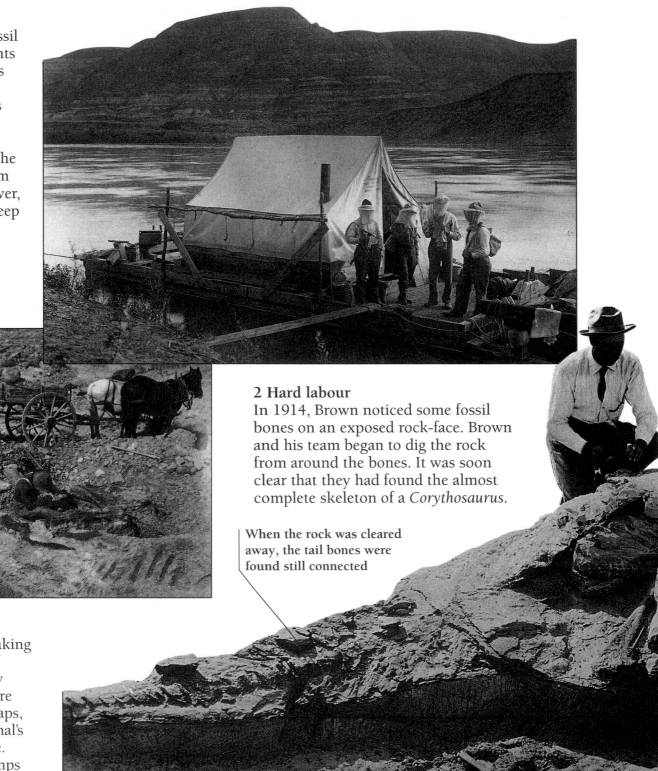

**1 Hunter's camp**
Far from any town, the fossil hunters had to sleep in tents on the river-bank. Life was harsh, and the men often wore nets over their heads to protect them from mosquito bites. All meals were cooked in a tent on the flatboat. Each day, the team sailed further down the river, stopping to explore the steep canyons that led off along the river-banks.

**2 Hard labour**
In 1914, Brown noticed some fossil bones on an exposed rock-face. Brown and his team began to dig the rock from around the bones. It was soon clear that they had found the almost complete skeleton of a *Corythosaurus*.

When the rock was cleared away, the tail bones were found still connected

**3 Fossil discovery**
After months of back-breaking work, the fragile fossils of *Corythosaurus* were finally uncovered. The fossils were riddled with cracks and gaps, but the shapes of the animal's limbs and tail were visible. Still partly attached to lumps of rock, the crumbling bones were carefully painted with glue to preserve their shape.

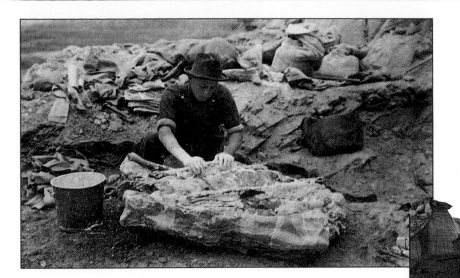

**5 Heavy fossils**
The huge blocks of rock and plaster containing the *Corythosaurus* skeleton were too heavy to lift by hand. Wooden beams, ropes, and pulleys were used to lift the massive blocks, lower them into strong, straw-lined crates, and then load them on to horse-drawn wagons.

**4 Broken bones**
Each block of rock containing the fragile fossils was wrapped in a protective jacket of sacking soaked in plaster. When the plaster was dry, the fossils were ready to begin the long journey to the Museum in New York.

**6 Wagon train**
The difficult journey by horse and cart to the railway often took many days. Many tonnes of fossils were carried in this way over the rough, barren landscape.

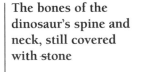

The bones of the dinosaur's spine and neck, still covered with stone

Part of the dinosaur's skeleton still lies buried

The arm bones have been well preserved, but parts of the hand were lost before the animal's carcase was buried

Hind leg of *Corythosaurus*

The bones of the right leg and foot partly conceal those on the other side

**7 Skeleton restoration**
Back at the Museum in New York, scientists first removed the plaster jackets from the broken bones, then glued them together and filled the gaps with plaster. Years of work were needed to transform the fossil fragments into an almost perfect dinosaur skeleton.

# SKELETON STORY

The almost complete skeleton of *Corythosaurus* that Barnum Brown had excavated, was finally placed on display at the American Museum of Natural History in New York after many years of painstaking restoration. Each fossil bone had to be chipped free of its stony jacket, repaired with plaster, and strengthened with glue. The huge, 7.5 m long (23 ft) skeleton was then put together and mounted in its original burial position in a large glass display case.

The skeleton can be recognized as *Corythosaurus* by its skull with a high, flat-sided crest, many rows of teeth, and horny beak. The powerful rear legs would have helped even a large, adult *Corythosaurus* to run quite swiftly over short distances, to escape from a prowling predator.

Short, slender arms ended in hands shaped like hooves for walking

**Death of a dinosaur**
Lying on its side, the mounted skeleton captures the moment, millions of years ago, when sand and mud covered the dead body of *Corythosaurus*. The legs, arms, and body shape have been preserved almost undisturbed in the dinosaur's original death pose.

There were over 60 vertebrae in the tail

Missing parts of the tail may have been washed away by floodwaters before the carcase was buried

**Bony corset**
Like all bird-hipped dinosaurs, *Corythosaurus* had extra scaffolding supporting its body. Long, bony rods, formed from muscle and tendons, criss-crossed along its back-bone, over the hips, and into the tail. This bony corset helped *Corythosaurus* to walk upright on two legs, but also held its tail stiff, so that it did not swing from side to side.

The long shaft of the ischium (rear hip bone) pointed backwards far under the tail. This helped to support some of the soft, internal organs

The large, three-toed feet ended in flattened hooves

The stiff, straight tail helped to balance the dinosaur's body when moving on two legs

Flat-sided, rounded crest of bone

*Corythosaurus* held the main part of its body parallel to the ground

### Two legs or four

A light, young *Corythosaurus* could walk easily on its hind legs, but a fully grown, heavy adult would have spent much of its time on all fours. When an adult *Corythosaurus* needed to escape an attacker, it could lift up its front limbs and run off quickly on its back legs.

19 vertebrae with tall spines supported the muscles and tendons along *Corythosaurus*' back

Bones that normally formed the snout of a dinosaur grew all the way back over *Corythosaurus*' head to form the crest

Scapula (shoulder blade)

Toothless beak

Femur (thigh bone)

Packed rows of grinding teeth

Curving neck with 15 vertebrae

Humerus (upper arm bone)

Deep ribcage

Tibia and fibula (shin bones)

Only a few of the finger bones were found fossilized

Radius and ulna (forearm bones)

# GREEDY GRAZER

During the Late Cretaceous Period, hadrosaurs like the 4-tonne (4-ton) *Corythosaurus* were among the most common dinosaurs of their day. Walking and running on stout limbs, the duck-bills travelled in large, fast-moving herds far across the coastal plains of what is now North America. These hungry plant-eaters munched their way through forest after forest of pine trees, ferns, flowers, and broad-leaved trees. Their rows of tightly packed teeth could mash even the toughest of twigs into soft pulp, which was then easy to swallow and digest.

**1 Reaching for food**
*Corythosaurus'* hooved fingers are shaped for walking, although it can use its hands and arms to pull branches towards its mouth.

The favourite food of *Corythosaurus* may have been trees like conifers and sycamores

**3 Grinding up food**
*Corythosaurus* leans forward with its beak to snip off a twig. Its jaws squeeze the food between its rows of teeth and grind it up.

The fossilized remains of seeds, fruits, pine needles, and twigs have all been found in the stomach of one mummified hadrosaur

**2 Feasting in the forest**
Ducking its head, *Corythosaurus* sweeps through the bushes, feeding mostly on plants up to 2 m (6.5 ft) tall. It rears up on its hind legs to strip off twigs, fruit, and leaves from the taller trees.

*Corythosaurus* may
have been able to run
fast because its tail
did not swing from
side to side and
slow it down

A heavy adult *Corythosaurus*
would most often stand and
walk on all fours. But at the
first sign of danger, it would
rise on its back legs, with
tail and body held straight,
and run off at the speed of
32 km/h (20 mph)

## Winter fodder
Remains of *Corythosaurus* have been found as far
north as present-day Alaska. Few plants would
have grown here in winter, so *Corythosaurus* may
have migrated south to warmer areas, in search
of fresh food to satisfy its monster appetite.

## 4 Moving off
*Corythosaurus* stands upright
to strip the last branches within
reach. The trees stand with torn
bark, and bare branches. It is
time to move on to new
feeding grounds.

No fossil evidence shows
the original skin colour of
*Corythosaurus*, but it may
have had striking markings
like some reptiles today

Scientists once thought
that *Corythosaurus*
had webbed hands.
It is now known that
each finger was
padded with a tough,
fleshy cushion

# SIGHT AND SMELL

The duck-bills, or hadrosaurs, are among the most easily identified of all the dinosaurs. Many of the species, including *Corythosaurus*, stood out with their spectacular head crests and distinctive mouths. *Corythosaurus'* sharp, rough-edged beak was made up of horn over bone, which grew throughout the animal's life, like human fingernails. The dinosaur's interlocking rows of teeth were also constantly replaced, with new teeth growing up from the jaw as old ones wore down. As a group, the hadrosaur family probably had highly developed senses of sight, smell, and hearing. These helped them pick up messages from other dinosaurs, such as warnings of danger.

**Dinosaur senses**
Although the brain of *Corythosaurus* seems small for such a large animal, it was well developed. It controlled the senses of sight, smell, and hearing as well as other body functions.

Chamber with smell-detecting part of the brain

Air passage to crest

Brain connected to smell organs

Nostrils let air into the hollow crest

**Flat-sided skulls**
The skull of *Hypacrosaurus* is easily mistaken for its relative *Corythosaurus*, but it has a less rounded crest. The skulls of both animals were long and flat-sided, rather like that of a horse.

Thin, hollow crest was made up of bones growing up from the nose to the back of the skull

Long, deep hollows on both sides of the skull led to the nostrils

The wide, bony snout of the living dinosaur was covered with horn, like a duck's beak

Hundreds of teeth were packed together to make long rasping surfaces, like files, in each jaw

As the lower jaws shut, they pushed each side of the upper jaws outwards. This caused the teeth to rub together from side to side to grind up food

## Dinosaur vision

Many predators have eyes that face forwards, giving them good vision for hunting or for using their hands.

Like many plant-eating animals, *Corythosaurus* had large eyes on the sides of its head. It could see in two different directions at once and watch for danger over a wide area as it fed.

Scientists do not know, however, if *Corythosaurus* saw in colour, as people do, or in shades of grey.

*Corythosaurus* would have seen two separate views of its surroundings at the same time. Its brain made sense of the different view from each side of its head

The left eye sees a *Euoplocephalus* feeding in the vegetation

The right eye sees danger from a hungry, prowling *Albertosaurus*

Left eye

Right eye

## Head signals

Hadrosaurs may have been able to recognize family members from the colour markings on their heads and from the differently shaped skulls. They communicated by using the air chambers in their crests to make distinctive hoots and calls.

The bony crest was covered in skin and may have been highly patterned to help hadrosaurs recognize others from the same group

All *Corythosaurus* crests were flat-sided, but some were smaller than others. Males may have had larger crests than females

A large eardrum at the back of the head helped *Corythosaurus* to pick up the calls made by other dinosaurs in the area

# HORNBLOWERS

Few living animals can compete with the amazing head crests sported by the hadrosaur family. Scientists once thought that hadrosaur crests were used as underwater snorkels and air-tanks, or that they helped the dinosaurs to smell an approaching attacker. It is now believed that the dinosaurs' crests may have helped them to identify one another. Hadrosaurs could tell males from females, and young dinosaurs from old, by the distinctive size and shape of their crests.

In recent experiments, scientists have tried blowing air through tubes similar to those in hollow hadrosaur crests. Results show that some duck-bills could also use their crests to call to one another.

The flat, head-plate was used to make hooting sounds

Spike at the back of the skull

Toothless beak

**Lambeosaurus skull**
Lambeosaurus may have used the flat-sided, hollow crest on top of its head to make sounds to communicate with other hadrosaurs. There was also a bony prong at the back of its skull.

**Kritosaurus**
Few remains have been found of the duck-bill Kritosaurus. It had no crest, except for a small, bony lump in front of its eyes.

Bony lump

**Lambeosaurus**
Lambeosaurus lived in North America at the same time as Corythosaurus. It had a distinctive hollow head crest.

**Edmontosaurus**
Edmontosaurus had no crest, but it may have had an inflatable skin balloon over its long snout, with which to make sounds. Many skulls have been found in the USA and Canada.

Inflatable skin balloon

**Parasaurolophus skull**
The skull of *Parasaurolophus* ended in a long, hollow crest. *Parasaurolophus* could use its crest to make loud noises. Animals could be told apart by their distinctive honks or hoots. Females and the young had smaller crests.

The crest contained hollow tubes and was 1 m long (over 3 ft)

Some scientists think that a flap of skin may have hung down from the end of the crest

Air tubes grew from the nostrils over the top of the skull

**Musical creatures**
Many animals have crests or flaps of skin to frighten or attract other animals. Some birds have brightly coloured feather crests, to signal to others of their kind. A few lizards and frogs can inflate a pouch of skin on their throat to attract a mate, or to make croaking noises.

The inflatable balloon of some hadrosaurs may have acted like the throat pouch of a bullfrog. Sounds made in a bullfrog's throat are made louder in its pouch and so can be heard far away

Inflated throat pouch

Rows of teeth for grinding up food

**Parasaurolophus**
*Parasaurolophus* had one of the longest hadrosaur crests. It contained two long, bony tubes that led up from the nostrils.

Bony spike

The hollow crests and air pouches of hadrosaurs varied in size and length. When calling in a group, these dinosaurs may have produced a range of honks and hoots

**Saurolophus**
*Saurolophus* may have had inflatable nostrils growing up from its snout. Remains have been found in North America and Mongolia.

Medieval horn

Musicians blow air through the tubes of differently shaped wind instruments to produce sounds, from low rumbles, to high whistling notes. Hadrosaurs may have made similar sounds, and the dinosaur world was probably quite noisy

# DINOSAUR MUMMY

In August 1908, George and Levi Sternberg, brothers from a family of dinosaur hunters, made an amazing discovery in the sandstone hills of Wyoming, USA. They unearthed the first fossilized dinosaur mummy ever found – an *Edmontosaurus*, still wrapped in the impression of its skin. Hot weather had dried its body, which was then buried, and slowly turned into fossil.

In 1912, four years after the Sternberg's find, Barnum Brown found the skin-covered fossil skeleton of a *Corythosaurus*, near the Red Deer River in Alberta, Canada. This body had not been mummified, but had been buried in a river-bed before it could decay. Both finds have helped research on duck-billed dinosaurs.

**Dinosaur skin to fossil impression**
The carcase of the *Corythosaurus* specimen found by Brown was probably washed away by floods and left stranded on a sandbank in a river. As the waters subsided, deep layers of sand and silt settled on top of the dead dinosaur.

The dinosaur carcase was not eaten by scavengers. The soft insides probably rotted away, but the bones, tendons, and tough skin survived long enough to be preserved as fossil

The thick blanket of river sand and silt that covered the dinosaur carcase kept the pattern and texture of its skin intact long enough to leave an impression on the rocks that formed around it

## Cousin of *Corythosaurus*

*Edmontosaurus* was another member of the duck-billed, or hadrosaur, family. Unlike *Corythosaurus*, it had a flat skull, but may have had an inflatable pouch of skin over its snout to make calling sounds. *Edmontosaurus* lived slightly later than *Corythosaurus* in the same area now known as North America and was one of the last surviving dinosaurs.

The dinosaur's soft flesh rotted away, leaving a perfect imprint in the surrounding rock. Over millions of years, chemicals in the hardening sand and silt slowly turned the buried *Corythosaurus* bones into stony fossils

## *Edmontosaurus* fossil mummy

The mummified *Edmontosaurus* was found by the Sternberg family in Niobrara County, Wyoming. It gave scientists the first evidence that dinosaur skin was similar to that of living reptiles. Today, it is on display at the AMNH in New York.

## Skin print

This fossilized impression, found by Barnum Brown, clearly shows that *Corythosaurus* skin was covered in a mosaic of small, pebbly bumps. But it cannot tell us about the colour markings on the dinosaur's body.

Dry heat made the tendons of the *Edmontosaurus* carcase shrink. As a result, the body twisted with its legs and ribs in the air, and its head pulled back behind the shoulders

65

# RIVERSIDE FEAST

About 78 million years ago, *Corythosaurus* foraged along a broad, flat plain, criss-crossed by swamps and rivers. This plain lay along the western shores of a great sea that washed from north to south across the middle of the land that is now called North America.

Many other plant-eating and meat-eating dinosaurs roamed through the vast forests with *Corythosaurus*. The plant-eaters fed on ferns, and trees such as conifers, cypresses, and flowering magnolias that flourished between the water-logged swamps and river channels.

**Dinosaur heaven**
The lush forests and rivers attracted many kinds of dinosaur. Plenty of plants grew to feed the herds of hungry herbivores, and there was a large supply of fresh water to drink. Lone meat-eaters, or carnivores, such as *Albertosaurus* prowled the area, hoping to catch a young or sickly plant-eater.

**Watching out for danger**
*Corythosaurus* may have had excellent senses of sight, smell, and hearing. At the first sign of danger from a predator, it could raise the alarm with a booming call from its high, crested head.

**Running away**
*Corythosaurus* enjoyed a diet of palm leaves, pine needles, fruits, and seeds. But at the first sign of a predator, it would quickly end its feast and rise up on its hind legs to escape.

Duck-bills may have paddled through the rivers and swamps, feeding on overhanging branches. Sometimes, the water may have been the only place to escape from an attacking predator

After the hadrosaurs, the horned dinosaurs were the second largest group by the riverside. Single-horned *Centrosaurus* could defend itself against attack with its sharp horns

Away from the river-bank, a group of *Lambeosaurus* would have watched nervously for the approach of a prowling *Albertosaurus*

**Ferocious hunter**
Fierce *Albertosaurus* hunted by the river. Its razor-sharp teeth could slash the soft flesh of its prey, the plant-eaters.

*Euoplocephalus* was well armoured against *Albertosaurus*

**Group defence**
*Chasmosaurus* used its long, sharp brow horns in defence against an *Albertosaurus*. In times of danger, a herd of *Chasmosaurus* might have formed a circle for protection and turned, horns outwards, to face their attacker.

**Poor swimmer**
In the past, researchers believed that *Corythosaurus* could swim by waving its tail to and fro in the water, like a crocodile. Fossil evidence shows that it could not swim as a cage of bony rods held the dinosaur's back and tail rigid.

A young *Corythosaurus* prepares to run for its life

# CORYTHOSAURUS SPECIMEN AND FAMILY FACTS

- **Specimen number:** AMNH 5338
- **Excavated by:** Barnum Brown
- **Excavation:** 1914, along the Red Deer River, near Steveville, Alberta, Canada
- **Bones found:** Almost complete skeleton, except for some hand and finger bones. Only about one-third of tail bones found

- **Where displayed:** American Museum of Natural History (AMNH), New York, USA
- **Constructed:** Mounted as a half skeleton at the AMNH and displayed in its original resting burial position.
  Plaster and glue used to repair and strengthen fossils

---

## 🏛 ON THE MUSEUM TRAIL 🏛
### A museum guide to hadrosaurid specimens

### EUROPE

**France**
(*Edmontosaurus*) National Museum of Natural History, Paris
**Germany**
(*Edmontosaurus*) Senckenberg Nature Museum, Frankfurt am Main
**United Kingdom**
(*Edmontosaurus, Parasaurolophus*) The Natural History Museum, London

### NORTH AMERICA

**USA**
(*Maiasaura*) Museum of the Rockies, Bozeman, Montana
(*Edmontosaurus*) Peabody Museum of Natural History, Yale University, Connecticut
(*Corythosaurus, Edmontosaurus, Lambeosaurus, Saurolophus*) American Museum of Natural History, New York
(*Corythosaurus*) Carnegie Museum of Natural History, Pittsburgh, Pennsylvania
(*Corythosaurus, Edmontosaurus*) National Museum of Natural History, Smithsonian Institution, Washington, DC

**Canada**
(*Corythosaurus, Edmontosaurus, Kritosaurus, Lambeosaurus, Parasaurolophus, Prosaurolophus*) Royal Ontario Museum, Toronto, Ontario
(*Corythosaurus, Hadrosaurus, Hypacrosaurus, Lambeosaurus, Maiasaura, Prosaurolophus*) Tyrrell Museum of Paleontology, Drumheller, Alberta

**Cased dinosaur**
*Corythosaurus* is displayed at the AMNH in its original death pose.

*Corythosaurus* had a strange helmeted head. It lived about 78 million years ago in North America

## Around the world

Hadrosaurid dinosaurs have been found in North and South America, Europe, and Asia. They lived as far north as Alaska and as far south as Argentina. This map shows where some members of the hadrosaur family have been found.

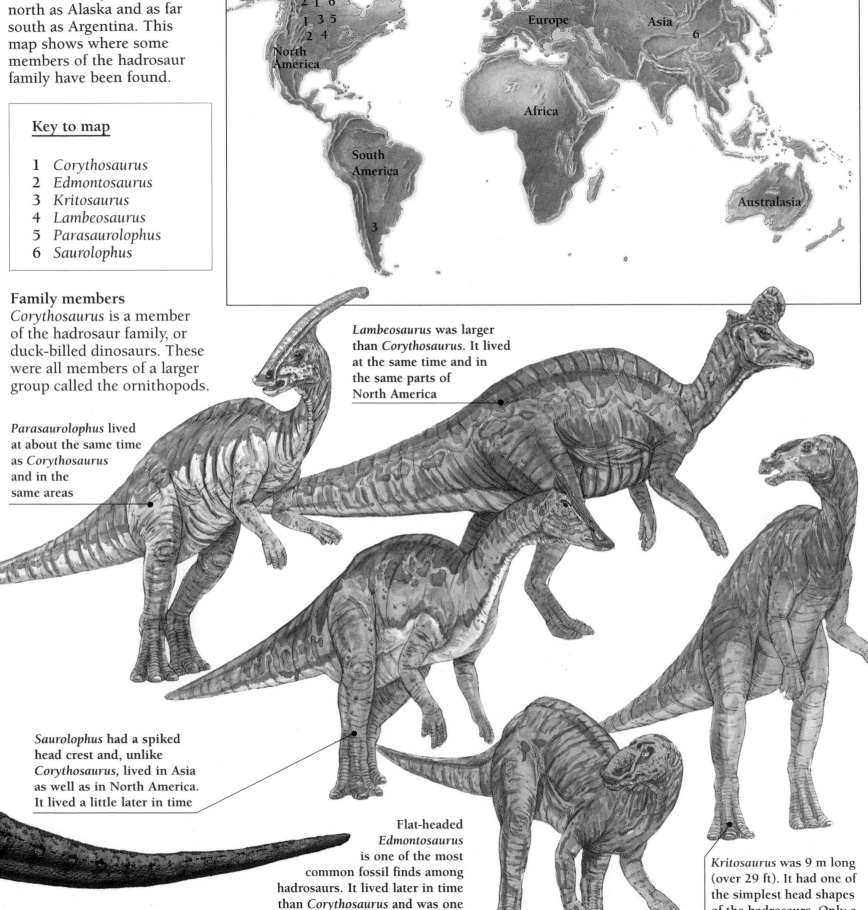

### Key to map

1 *Corythosaurus*
2 *Edmontosaurus*
3 *Kritosaurus*
4 *Lambeosaurus*
5 *Parasaurolophus*
6 *Saurolophus*

## Family members

*Corythosaurus* is a member of the hadrosaur family, or duck-billed dinosaurs. These were all members of a larger group called the ornithopods.

*Parasaurolophus* lived at about the same time as *Corythosaurus* and in the same areas

*Lambeosaurus* was larger than *Corythosaurus*. It lived at the same time and in the same parts of North America

*Saurolophus* had a spiked head crest and, unlike *Corythosaurus,* lived in Asia as well as in North America. It lived a little later in time

Flat-headed *Edmontosaurus* is one of the most common fossil finds among hadrosaurs. It lived later in time than *Corythosaurus* and was one of the last duck-bills living in North America. It was 13 m in length (over 49 ft)

*Kritosaurus* was 9 m long (over 29 ft). It had one of the simplest head shapes of the hadrosaurs. Only a bump in front of its eyes stood out on its flat head

# TRICERATOPS

*Triceratops* was one of the last dinosaurs to walk the Earth. It lived at the end of the Cretaceous Period and shared its world with *Tyrannosaurus rex*, the ferocious meat-eater. Did the large, bony head-frill and long horns of *Triceratops* protect it from this terrifying attacker? Possibly, but we do not know for sure. *Triceratops* and other horned dinosaurs, or ceratopsids, have different shapes and sizes of horns and frills. It seems most likely that the horns were used for defence, and the large frills for display.

The shape of the horns and head-frills varies quite a lot between different individual *Triceratops*. The horns above the eyes are sometimes curved forwards and sometimes straight, and some frills are flatter than others. Until quite recently, scientists divided *Triceratops* into thirteen different species based on these differences. Now it has been recognized that there is one or maybe two species of *Triceratops*. The shapes and sizes of horns and frills vary between individuals in just the same way that some of our features do.

*Triceratops* and other horned dinosaurs were plant-eaters with sharp beaks and scissor-like teeth. Like many plant-eaters, they lived in herds. One fossil site in Canada has revealed the remains of a herd of more than 1,000 horned dinosaur babies and adults that were washed away while trying to cross a flooded river. Similar accidents happen to plant-eating herds such as caribou and wildebeest today.

# THREE-HORNED FACE

*Triceratops*, with its huge horns and bony head-frill, was one of the last surviving dinosaurs. Sixty-five million years after its death, scientists are able to piece together information gathered from clues left behind and learn how this dinosaur lived. *Triceratops* is one of the most common dinosaurs to be found in western North America. Fossil hunters have collected the remains of more than 1,500 *Triceratops* – although few of these are complete skeletons. Finding a complete skeleton of any dinosaur, even of a common one, such as *Triceratops*, is a rare and thrilling event.

*Iguanodon* "bird-hipped" dinosaur

**Horned family**
*Triceratops* belongs to the group of horned dinosaurs called the ceratopsids. Their large horns and strong bodies were a good defence against predators.

*Triceratops* (try-ser-rah-tops) means "three-horned face"

**Bird-hipped**
*Triceratops* was a "bird-hipped" or ornithischian dinosaur. The two lower bones of its pelvis pointed backwards and down.

*Triceratops* had a huge, frilled crest that extended from the back of its skull and doubled the size of its head

*Triceratops* was armed with long, stabbing nose and eyebrow horns

**Changing Earth**

*Triceratops* lived right at the end of the Cretaceous Period, at the same time as the ferocious *Tyrannosaurus rex*.

| TRIASSIC PERIOD | JURASSIC PERIOD | CRETACEOUS PERIOD |
|---|---|---|
| 248–205 million years ago | 205–145 million years ago | 145–65 million years ago |

The frills of some *Triceratops* have holes punched right through the bone. It has been suggested that these may be punctures made by the horn tips during combat with other *Triceratops*

**Plant-eater**
Like other ceratopsids, *Triceratops* was a plant-eater, or herbivore. It had a sharp, toothless beak to slice through tough leaves and twigs.

*Triceratops* weighed as much as a fully grown African elephant. Its great bulk was supported by four sturdy legs

**FACT FILE**
- **Lived:** 67–65 million years ago, during the Late Cretaceous Period
- **Family:** Ceratopsids, the horned dinosaurs
- **Dinosaur type:** Bird-hipped (ornithischian)
- **Diet:** Plants
- **Weight when alive:** 6 tonnes (over 6 tons)
- **Height:** 3 m (over 9 ft)
- **Length:** Up to 9 m (over 29 ft)
- **Top speed:** Perhaps about 25 km/h (15 mph)

# BURIED TREASURE

Only the skull survives of a *Triceratops* that died 65 million years ago. The rest of the dinosaur's bones may have been eaten by animals or swept away by floods. The skull was buried in the mud and sand of a river-bed where it was slowly turned into stony fossil.

The skull was discovered in 1909 at Seven Mile Creek, Niobrara County, Wyoming, USA, by the American fossil hunter, George Sternberg, and his family. Parts of another *Triceratops* were found in the same year by Barnum Brown at Hell Creek, Montana, USA.

**Fossil world**
The *Triceratops* skull found in 1909 is the only part left of this dinosaur. Buried underground, the skull was slowly turned as hard as stone by the chemicals in the surrounding rock.

**1 Living dinosaur**
65 million years ago, *Triceratops* sips water from a rushing river. The river flows past prehistoric trees and plants such as monkey puzzles, willows, conifers, palms, and ferns.

**2 Bare bones**
A few years on, *Triceratops* has died from old age or disease. Its bones have been picked clean by meat-eaters and now lie on the bank of a dried-up river-bed.

**3 Buried skull**
*Triceratops*' skull lies buried in the mud and sand of the river-bed. The rest of the skeleton has been destroyed by animals, plants, and the weather.

## DINOSAUR DETECTIVE
### George Sternberg (1883 – 1969)

George Sternberg was the eldest of Charles Sternberg's three sons. He was first taken fossil collecting at the age of six, and continued to work on fossils for another 66 years. With his father and brothers, George Sternberg discovered some of the most amazing fossil treasures ever found in North America.

| | |
|---|---|
| 1883 | *Born at Lawrence, Kansas, USA.* |
| 1908 | *Discovered the first known fossil of a mummified dinosaur, a duck-bill called* **Edmontosaurus**, *with his brother Levi.* |
| 1909 | *Discovered a fine skull of* **Triceratops**, *with his father and brothers.* |
| 1952 | *Discovered the fossil of a 4 m (14 ft) long prehistoric fish, containing a fish almost 2 m (6 ft) long, that it had eaten before it died.* |
| 1969 | *Died on 23 October at Hays, Kansas, aged 86.* |
| 1970 | *The fossil collection at Fort Hays State University, Kansas, founded by George Sternberg, was officially designated the Sternberg Museum.* |

*Friendly fossil hunters*
*The Sternbergs visit their fellow dinosaur hunter, Barnum Brown, on a fossil-collecting expedition.*

**Bone and horn**
Now preserved as a hard, stony fossil, the brow horn of *Triceratops* was once a living bone. During the animal's lifetime, the bone was encased in a layer of horn, ending in a sharp tip. Grooves in the surface of the fossil show where the bone was once fed by a pattern of blood vessels.

**Tracing *Triceratops***
Remains of *Triceratops* have been found in several sites in North America, in rocks formed during the Cretaceous Period of the Earth's history. Barnum Brown discovered his specimens near Hell Creek, Montana, USA, while the Sternberg's skull came from further south, along a riverside in Niobrara County, Wyoming. Many of the best fossil specimens of *Triceratops* have come from this area.

Seven Mile Creek, Wyoming

Discovery site of the *Triceratops* skull

**6 Fossil find**
Centuries of wind and rain have worn the rocks of the ancient river-bed into barren hills and steep-sided canyons. The weather has also exposed parts of the *Triceratops* skull, which now lies waiting to be discovered.

**4 Stony fossil**
15 million years after the death of *Triceratops*, the dinosaurs have died out and mammals have taken over the Earth. Chemicals have slowly turned the mud and sand of the old river-bed into rock, and the buried skull into hard, stony fossil.

**5 Icy grave**
15,000 years ago, the land lies frozen in an Ice Age. Earth movements have pushed up the fossil skull in its rocky layer, together with a new range of mountains.

# FOSSIL FRAGMENTS

In 1909, the Sternberg family were hunting for fossils on behalf of the American Museum of Natural History (AMNH) in New York. The Sternbergs found a fine example of a *Triceratops* skull in the barren hills of Wyoming, USA. They cleared away tonnes of rock to expose the ancient dinosaur remains.

The fossils were packed up and shipped to New York. At the AMNH, scientists carefully restored the *Triceratops* skull. The skull was then mounted, together with remains from at least four different *Triceratops* animals, to create a free-standing fossil skeleton for display in the Museum's world-famous dinosaur hall.

Charles Sternberg chisels out the skull of a horned dinosaur

## 2 Fossil discovery
In 1909, George Sternberg noticed fossil fragments emerging from a steep hillside. He and his brothers began to chip away the stone around the fragile dinosaur bones, using hammers, picks, and chisels. The Sternbergs slowly uncovered the shattered remains of a *Triceratops* skull.

## 1 Barren hunting ground
The Sternbergs came to hunt fossils in the rugged badlands of Wyoming, where ancient rocks have been weathered into flat-topped hills and steep-sided canyons. The dinosaur hunters looked for fragments of fossil, tell-tale clues to treasures buried in the hillsides.

The *Triceratops* skull was found lying upside-down

## 3 Dinosaur graveyard
One year earlier, the Sternbergs had uncovered fossil remains of another *Triceratops* in the same area as their new find. The sandstone rock layers of Wyoming proved to be a dinosaur graveyard, rich in fossil treasures.

## 4 Surviving skull
Only the *Triceratops* skull had survived as a fossil. The other dinosaur bones had been destroyed before they could be buried. Once the Sternbergs had cleared the rock away from the fossil, they sifted the debris to collect up any missing pieces of the badly broken frill.

## 5 Plaster jackets
The fragile fossil bones needed to be well protected in transit to the AMNH. First, the fossils were covered in a protective layer of thin paper. Next, the bones were wrapped in sacking soaked in plaster.

The supportive plaster jacket held the shattered fossil bones together

## 6 Heavy load
When the plaster had dried, the heavy blocks containing the sections of skull were hoisted into strong wooden crates. At last the *Triceratops* skull was ready to begin its long journey to New York.

Glue and plaster were used to mend the cracked fossils

## 7 Horse and cart
Horses were used to drag the wooden crates out of the fossil quarry. At the top of the slope, the boxes were loaded on to a horse-drawn cart and dragged across rough country to the nearest railway.

## 8 Skull restoration
Back at the AMNH, scientists needed great skill to repair the skull as the shattered frill had to be rebuilt from many pieces. The *Triceratops* skull was supported on a metal rod and wooden props while it was slowly pieced together.

The small, bony knobs from along the edge of the frill had not been found and were not replaced

# SKULL AND BONES

After several years of preparation, the *Triceratops* skull found by the Sternbergs and the skeleton found by Barnum Brown were finally ready for display at the American Museum of Natural History. *Triceratops* was one of the strongest dinosaurs. Its massive horned skull and nearly 9 m (over 29 ft) long, barrel-like body were built to withstand attack from the fiercest predator. Some scientists believe that *Triceratops* could have charged at more than 25 km/h (almost 15 mph), against an attacking meat-eater.

**Crash barrier**
The thick skull and strongly built neck and hips of *Triceratops* all helped it to withstand the impact of crashing into an attacker or locking horns with a rival. *Triceratops* could also charge quickly over short distances on its powerful legs. It would not have been easy prey, even for the huge meat-eating dinosaurs such as *Tyrannosaurus rex*.

Skin-covered bony frill edged with a rim of bony studs

Brow horn, about 1 m (over 3 ft) long

Short nose horn

Eyes were set in deep, well-protected sockets

**Huge head**
The enormous head of *Triceratops* made up almost one-third of its overall length. The head was armed with long, sharp horns on the brow and nose. The head-frill was edged with bony lumps and protected the dinosaur's powerful neck. The bony horns would have been longer in life when they were covered with a layer of horn.

Powerful jaws were operated by huge muscles stretching down from the frill

Rows of teeth for slicing food

Humerus (upper arm bones)

Ulna and radius (forearm bones)

**Front and back view**
The high, wide frill and long horns added to the threatening size of *Triceratops*' head. Sturdy, strong legs gave *Triceratops* great strength when facing an attacker.

The horns could be used as fearsome weapons if they did not scare off an attacker

Ten back vertebrae gave strength and rigidity to the pelvis

The sharp-edged, horny beak was used to snip off tough leaves and branches

Back vertebrae

**Tail position**
Dinosaurs probably walked with their tails held above the ground. Dinosaur footprints left fossilized in mud show no marks left by dragging tails. In the past, however, scientists often mounted skeletons with tails brushing the ground.

Pubis (lower pelvic bone)

The upper pelvic bone anchored the leg muscles, while the two lower pelvic bones supported and protected the soft internal organs

Ischium (lower pelvic bone)

There were probably over 30 vertebrae in the tail of *Triceratops*

Long curved ribs gave *Triceratops* a deep-chested, stocky body

Femur (thigh bone)

Tibia (shin bone)

Short front legs and longer rear legs were stout pillars of bone

Four broad toes on the rear feet and five toes on the front feet ended in hoof-like claws which helped spread the great weight of *Triceratops*

Fibula (leg bone)

# HUNGRY HERDERS

Triceratops was one of the most common dinosaurs living in the area now known as North America, 65 million years ago. Huge herds of horned plant-eaters roamed through the forests, along the banks of rivers and edges of swamps. The hordes of hungry dinosaurs fed on trees, shrubs, and ferns, and only tall plants were safe from the giant appetite of *Triceratops*.

**Flowering food**
*Triceratops* and the other plant-eaters of the time ate the new flowering plants, such as magnolia, oak, and laurel, that appeared during the Cretaceous Period. Grasslands did not appear until 40 million years after the dinosaurs died out.

**Snipping beak**
*Triceratops* used its sharp beak to snip off leaves and twigs that grew up to 3 m (9 ft) from the ground.

**Growing beak**
*Triceratops'* beak was worn down by its rough diet, but continued to grow throughout the dinosaur's lifetime, rather like human fingernails.

**Herbivores and hunters**
Many dinosaurs fed on the plants that grew on the lush plains. Fierce meat-eaters followed the herds, hunting young or sickly herbivores.

*Edmontosaurus*
The duck-billed dinosaur *Edmontosaurus* lived in a herd. It could reach leaves on tree branches that were out of *Triceratops*' reach.

*Pachycephalosaurus*
*Pachycephalosaurus* had a thick, domed head, ringed by bony spikes, but which gave no protection against a predator.

*Tyrannosaurus* **and** *Ornithomimus*
*Triceratops* had dangerously sharp horns to defend itself against fierce *Tyrannosaurus*. *Ornithomimus* was built like a modern-day ostrich and could have run away from any danger.

*Triceratops*

*Tyrannosaurus*

*Ornithomimus*

*Torosaurus*
*Torosaurus* had a huge, horned skull. It was always on the lookout for danger from an attacking predator.

**Migration**
*Triceratops* could only survive if it found enough to eat. During a drought, *Triceratops* and the other plant-eaters may have migrated long distances in search of new feeding-grounds.

**Jaws like shears**
*Triceratops*' tooth-lined jaws worked like garden shears. The dinosaur's jaws sliced up plants between its sharp-edged upper and lower teeth.

# HORNED DEFENCE

Triceratops was well protected against the fierce predators, such as Tyrannosaurus, that tracked the herds of plant-eaters across the great plain. Triceratops' giant, bony frill also made its head look huge and frightening to deter any prowling carnivore, or meat-eater. Triceratops had long, sharp horns on its forehead and snout. In addition, the dinosaur had specially strengthened bones in its neck and hip area and on the roof of its skull to withstand great shocks if it charged into an attacker.

**Attacking monster**
A hungry Tyrannosaurus spots a Triceratops, feeding away from its herd. The meat-eater rushes at its prey, hoping to knock it down. It will try to wound Triceratops with one fatal bite from its dagger-like teeth.

**Fighting back**
Triceratops shakes its head, bellows, and lunges towards its attacker. Charging forwards, Triceratops tries to stab the belly of its fearsome opponent with its horns. If it succeeds, Triceratops may escape from death – this time.

**Standing its ground**
Triceratops paws the ground and hisses at Tyrannosaurus, looking for a way to escape the terrible hunter's razor-sharp, slashing teeth. But Tyrannosaurus is growing tired and may decide to give up and hunt a weaker animal.

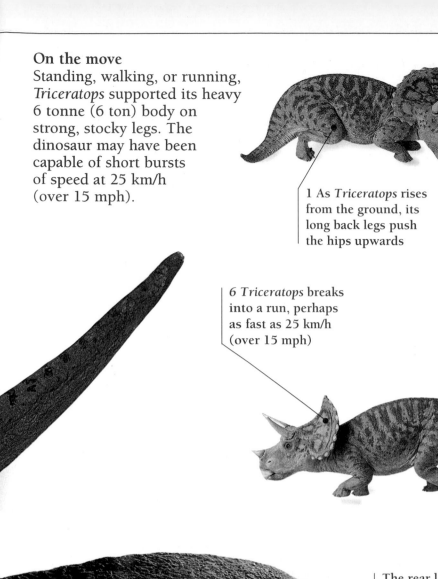

## On the move

Standing, walking, or running, *Triceratops* supported its heavy 6 tonne (6 ton) body on strong, stocky legs. The dinosaur may have been capable of short bursts of speed at 25 km/h (over 15 mph).

**3** Hip bones take the strain of *Triceratops'* heavy body weight

**1** As *Triceratops* rises from the ground, its long back legs push the hips upwards

**2** Huge muscles support *Triceratops'* great body over the front and rear legs

**6** *Triceratops* breaks into a run, perhaps as fast as 25 km/h (over 15 mph)

**4** *Triceratops* may have walked at speeds of around 10 km/h (over 6 mph)

**5** *Triceratops* catches sight of an attacker and prepares to charge

The rear legs are braced, ready for the impact with *Tyrannosaurus*

The legs kick up a cloud of dust to try and confuse the attacker

## Means of defence

*Triceratops* may look a little like a rhinoceros, but it was twice the size and a reptile, not a mammal. Nevertheless, the dinosaur may have had similar ways of defending itself. Some rhinos charge, while others stand in a defensive circle, horns pointing outwards from the group.

# DESERT ADVENTURES

In 1922, scientists from the American Museum of Natural History (AMNH) first travelled to the Gobi Desert of Mongolia in Central Asia. The expedition had set out to find fossil evidence of early humans. Instead, it was to make one of the most important discoveries ever about dinosaurs. In 1923, the team collected the first known dinosaur eggs and nest, together with fossil bones of *Protoceratops*, the horned dinosaur that was thought to have laid the eggs. Sixty years later, other scientists from the AMNH returned to the Gobi to find out more about dinosaurs and their young. They discovered the dinosaur nests and eggs belonged to a completely different dinosaur, *Oviraptor*.

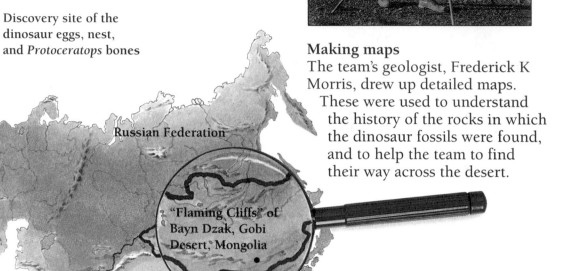

Discovery site of the dinosaur eggs, nest, and *Protoceratops* bones

Russian Federation

"Flaming Cliffs" of Bayn Dzak, Gobi Desert, Mongolia

China

India

**Making maps**
The team's geologist, Frederick K Morris, drew up detailed maps. These were used to understand the history of the rocks in which the dinosaur fossils were found, and to help the team to find their way across the desert.

**Dinosaur hunter**
Walter Granger was deputy leader on the AMNH expeditions to the Gobi, as well as the chief palaeontologist. Granger is seen here, delicately brushing sand and grit from a fossil.

**Finding the eggs**
On 13 July 1923, the assistant, George Olsen, came across three shattered fossil eggs and some dinosaur bones. Andrews and Granger realized that the team had discovered real proof that dinosaurs hatched from eggs, like other reptiles.

**Expedition leader**
Roy Chapman Andrews was the leader of the 1923 expedition. He had begun raising funds and planning the expedition several years earlier.

**Cars and camels**
Mongolian and Chinese scientists joined the American team on their five expeditions to the Gobi Desert in the 1920s. They travelled in large cars, and met up regularly with camel trains to collect fresh supplies of food and petrol.

**Asian cousin of *Triceratops***
*Protoceratops* was only 1 m to 2.5 m long (3 ft to over 8 ft), about the size of a small horse. *Protoceratops* lived about 85 million years ago, on the continent now called Asia. Its relatives, the horned dinosaurs, such as *Triceratops*, have mainly been found in North America.

*Protoceratops* had a beak, short frill, and wide cheek-bones. It had no horns, even though it was a member of the family of horned dinosaurs

**1 Planning an expedition**
Since the late 1980s, scientists from the AMNH have returned several times to the Gobi Desert. Before each trip, they check weather patterns, and plan routes and exploration sites with Mongolian colleagues, to allow as much time as possible for collecting fossils.

**2 Searching for clues**
The field leader, Mark Norell, studies debris on the dry desert floor. Fossils look shinier than the red sand and mudstone. Norell studies the fossils to decide whether it would be worth spending time searching for dinosaur remains in this area.

**3 Collecting samples**
A scientist collects samples of dinosaur bone from the crumbling, rocky cliffs. During the day, the desert is baking hot. At night, it can be freezing cold. Few plants grow here, and any rocks and bones exposed to the heat and cold are soon worn into dust.

**4 Excavating fossils**
The scientists work slowly to brush away the sand from around a dinosaur skull. They chip away any hard lumps of rock with small picks. The exposed fossil is then strengthened with a coating of glue.

**5 Packing up the fossils**
Once the glue is dry, each fossil is wrapped in a thin lining of paper, followed by sacking soaked in plaster. When the protective plaster layer has set hard, the fossil can be lifted and carried back to camp, ready to be shipped back for study at the AMNH.

# DINOSAUR BABIES

Since the discovery of fossil dinosaur eggs, nests, and bones in the Gobi Desert in 1923, similar finds have been made around the world. Scientists have been able to use these remains to work out how dinosaurs may have developed and how they tended their young. Most of the Gobi nests are now known to belong to *Oviraptor*, but perhaps *Protoceratops* nested in a similar way.

The many *Protoceratops* skeletons found range from tiny skeletons to fully grown adults. These bones show how *Protoceratops* changed in size and shape as it grew.

All these findings may offer clues to the lives of *Triceratops* and other horned dinosaurs, whose nests, eggs, and babies have not yet been found.

### Nesting sites

It is thought that *Protoceratops* probably scooped out a bowl-shaped nest in soft, dry sand – laying its eggs in a circle as it turned around in the nest. Many females may have nested at a single site – a large number of adults staying close together perhaps helped to keep predators away.

Like a modern-day reptile, a dinosaur would have laid its eggs from an opening under its tail, just behind the hip bones

It was once thought that an adult *Protoceratops* may have had to protect its eggs from nest-robbing dinosaurs such as *Oviraptor*. However, work by the AMNH scientists in the 1990's has shown that *Oviraptor* did not rob *Protoceratops*' nests. Adult *Oviraptor* have been found sitting on their own clutches of eggs – once thought to belong to *Protoceratops*.

### Hatching out

The baby *Protoceratops* cracked their eggs open from the inside. They may have used their tiny beaks to break through the shell, or burst through by flexing their muscles hard.

### Feeding the young

Soon after hatching, the baby *Protoceratops* would have stretched their legs and set off in search of food. The adults may have stayed close by to bring plants to the nest for the first few days.

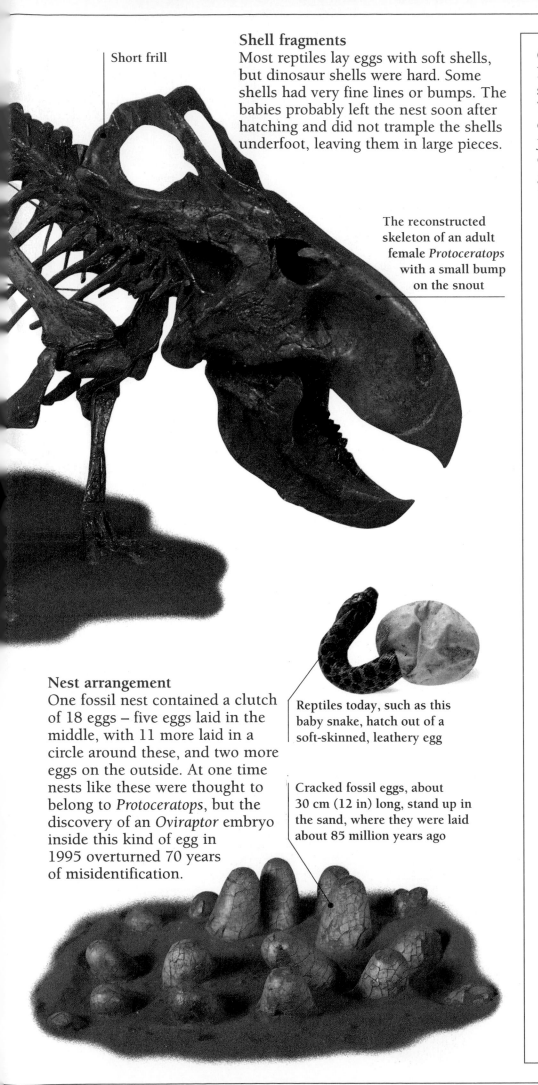

**Short frill**

### Shell fragments
Most reptiles lay eggs with soft shells, but dinosaur shells were hard. Some shells had very fine lines or bumps. The babies probably left the nest soon after hatching and did not trample the shells underfoot, leaving them in large pieces.

The reconstructed skeleton of an adult female *Protoceratops* with a small bump on the snout

### Growing up
Many *Protoceratops* skulls have been found. These show how the dinosaurs' skulls and jaws developed at different stages of growth, from hatching to adulthood.

The skull of a newly hatched *Protoceratops*

A *Protoceratops* baby has large eye sockets set in a small skull

The young *Protoceratops* starts to develop more of the features of an adult's skull

As *Protoceratops* grows older, its frill becomes larger and wider

Male and female *Protoceratops* may have developed different characteristics. This may be a male, with a wide frill and a smooth snout

The growing frill anchors *Protoceratops*' large jaw muscles. This gives the jaw the strength to slice through tough leaves and stems

### Nest arrangement
One fossil nest contained a clutch of 18 eggs – five eggs laid in the middle, with 11 more laid in a circle around these, and two more eggs on the outside. At one time nests like these were thought to belong to *Protoceratops*, but the discovery of an *Oviraptor* embryo inside this kind of egg in 1995 overturned 70 years of misidentification.

Reptiles today, such as this baby snake, hatch out of a soft-skinned, leathery egg

Cracked fossil eggs, about 30 cm (12 in) long, stand up in the sand, where they were laid about 85 million years ago

*Protoceratops* is almost fully grown. Its beak and snout have become narrower, and the back of the skull is wider

*Protoceratops* is now a fully developed adult. Its wide cheek bones and frill stand out from the skull

# HEAD-FRILLS AND HORNS

Spikes, lumps, fans, and frills decorated the heads of the family of horned dinosaurs, the ceratopsids. These features help scientists to distinguish one horned dinosaur from another, as few well-preserved skeletons have been found. Differences in the shape and size of skulls also helped the living dinosaurs to recognize one another and indicated whether an animal was male or female, young or old.

As well as providing armour against an attacking predator, the horns of this dinosaur family probably had an extra purpose. The ceratopsid dinosaurs may have used their horns against rivals to win territory or a mate, just as deer lock antlers today.

Some scientists believe that the head-frills and spikes of the living dinosaurs may have been highly coloured as a warning to predators or to attract a mate, but no fossil evidence survives to support this theory.

Large "windows" made the huge frill lighter, helping *Chasmosaurus* to raise and lower its head

*Chasmosaurus*

**Chasmosaurus**
Small spikes lined the rear and side edges of *Chasmosaurus'* frill.

Stout nose horn

*Centrosaurus*

Eye socket

The massive jaw muscles bulged through spaces in the side of the frill when *Centrosaurus* closed its jaws

Short frill

Sharp, toothless beak

**Centrosaurus**
*Centrosaurus* had a short frill, but only one horn, which grew high up over its nostrils. A curved spike pointed down and forwards above each opening in the frill.

*Styracosaurus*

"Window" in frill

Large nostril cavity

Bony prong

### Styracosaurus
*Styracosaurus* had a comb of six large, bony spines that stretched back from its frill, as well as a long, straight nose horn. A bony prong grew downwards from each cheek, along the edge of the lower jaw. Two large "windows" made the frill lighter, so that the dinosaur could move its head more easily.

Nose horn

Large, bony spine

Sharp beak covered with horn

*Pentaceratops*

Brow horn

"Window" in frill

Bony knobs on edge of frill

Nose horn

Extended cheek bone

### Pentaceratops
*Pentaceratops* is named after the five horns on its skull. However, only three of these are really horns – two on the brow, and one on the animal's snout. The other two are spiky cheek bones. A large frill also fanned out over the neck and shoulders of *Pentaceratops*.

# TRICERATOPS SPECIMEN AND FAMILY FACTS

- **Specimen numbers:** AMNH 5116, 5033, 5039, 5045
- **Excavated by:** The Sternberg family; Barnum Brown
- **Excavations:** Seven Mile Creek, Niobrara County, Wyoming, USA; Hell Creek, Montana, USA

- **Bones found:** Skull and most of the skeleton, except for the front limbs; the composite skeleton is made up of the remains of at least four separate animals
- **Where displayed:** American Museum of Natural History (AMNH), New York, USA

## 🏛 ON THE MUSEUM TRAIL 🏛

### A museum guide to ceratopsid specimens

#### EUROPE

**France**
(*Protoceratops, Triceratops*) National Museum of Natural History, Institute of Palaeontology, Paris

**Germany**
(*Protoceratops, Triceratops*) Senckenberg Nature Museum, Frankfurt am Main
(*Centrosaurus, Triceratops*) Bavarian State Institute for Paleontology and Historical Geology, Munich
(*Protoceratops*) Institute and Museum for Geology and Paleontology, University of Tübingen, Tübingen

**Spain**
(*Protoceratops*) Natural Science Museum, Madrid

**Sweden**
(*Pentaceratops*) Paleontological Museum, Uppsala University, Uppsala

**United Kingdom**
(*Triceratops*) Birmingham Museum, Dept of Natural History, Birmingham
(*Centrosaurus, Protoceratops, Triceratops*) Natural History Museum, London
(*Triceratops*) Hunterian Museum, The University, Glasgow
(*Triceratops*) Royal Museum of Scotland, Edinburgh

#### USA

(*Centrosaurus, Montanoceratops, Protoceratops, Styracosaurus, Triceratops*) American Museum of Natural History, New York
(*Protoceratops*) Carnegie Museum of Natural History, Pittsburgh, Pennsylvania
(*Centrosaurus, Triceratops*) National Museum of Natural History, Smithsonian Institution, Washington, DC

The *Triceratops* skeleton on display at the AMNH was made up from the fossil remains of at least four different animals

*Triceratops* was one of the last dinosaurs on Earth. Its huge horns and giant frill made this large dinosaur look even bigger

## Changing world

This map shows areas in which horned dinosaurs have been discovered. Although *Triceratops* is one of the most common dinosaurs to be found, its remains and those of other horned dinosaurs have been found only on the continents of North America and Asia.

### Key to map

1 *Chasmosaurus*
2 *Centrosaurus*
3 *Pentaceratops*
4 *Styracosaurus*
5 *Torosaurus*
6 *Triceratops*
7 *Protoceratops*

## The horned dinosaur family

*Triceratops* was a member of the chasmosaurines, one of two groups of horned dinosaurs. The other group, the centrosaurines, had shorter head-frills and longer nose horns. Together they belonged to the ceratopsid family.

A long-frilled horned dinosaur, *Pentaceratops* was about the same size as *Triceratops*. It became extinct just before *Triceratops* appeared

*Torosaurus* had the largest skull of the horned dinosaurs, but fossil remains of its limbs and body have not yet been found. *Torosaurus* also lived in the Cretaceous Period and in the same part of the world as *Triceratops*

*Chasmosaurus* lived about 75 million years ago. Its fossil remains have been found in Alberta, Canada, and in Texas, USA

*Centrosaurus* was over 5 m (18 ft) long and lived 75 million years ago in the land that is now known as North America

*Styracosaurus* had long horns and a short frill. It lived earlier than *Triceratops* and, like most horned dinosaurs, has been found in North America

*Protoceratops* is the only horned dinosaur to have been found so far in Central Asia. It was the size of a small horse

91

# GLOSSARY

**carcase**
The body of a dead animal.

**carnivore**
A meat-eating animal.

**carnosaur**
A group of dinosaurs that were the largest meat-eaters to have lived on land.

**cast**
A replica of a fossil, made from a mould of the original.

**ceratopsids**
Family of horned dinosaurs. There were two groups of ceratopsids: the chasmosaurines and the centrosaurines. *Triceratops* was a member of the chasmosaurines.

**composite skeleton**
A skeleton made up of parts from more than one incomplete specimen.

**crest**
A decoration of feathers, skin, or bone growing on top of an animal's head; used by an animal to signal to other animals of its kind.

**Cretaceous Period**
Part of the Earth's history that lasted from 145 million years ago until the dinosaurs died out 65 million years ago. *Tyrannosaurus rex* lived during this period.

**dinosaurs**
A group of extinct, land-living reptiles that lived on Earth from 230 to 65 million years ago.

**duck-billed dinosaur**
Another name for a hadrosaur, a dinosaur with a duck-like beak.

**environment**
The land, water, and climate that surrounds living things and affects how they live.

**excavate**
To dig up an object such as a fossil.

**extinction**
When living things, such as dinosaurs, die out and disappear from the Earth forever.

**formation**
An arrangement of rock layers formed over millions of years.

**fossil**
Part of a dead plant or animal that has been buried and turned as hard as stone by chemicals in the rock.

**gastrolith**
A stone swallowed by a dinosaur and used in part of its stomach to help grind up tough plants.

**glass fibre**
A fine mat of glass threads, which is used to strengthen plastic for fossil casts.

**hadrosaur**
Another name for a duck-billed dinosaur, such as *Corythosaurus*.

**head-frill**
The wide rim of bone that fans out from the back of the skull of a horned dinosaur.

**herbivore**
A plant-eating animal.

**horns**
Sharp, pointed features that grew on the skulls of horned dinosaurs. They were made of material like that of human fingernails, growing over a bony core.

**impression**
A copy of the shape and surface markings of a fossil.

**Jurassic Period**
Part of the Earth's history from 205 to 145 million years ago, when large plant-eating sauropod dinosaurs were common.

**mammal**
An animal that has hair-covered skin, gives birth to live young, and feeds them with milk.

**mosaic**
A pattern made up of small lumps or pieces.

**mould**
The impression of an original object from which a cast is made.

**mummy**
A carcase that has been dried out by natural or chemical means before being buried, and so preserved from rotting.

**organ**
A soft part inside an animal's body, such as the heart or stomach.

**ornithischian dinosaur**
The bird-hipped type of dinosaur with both lower hip bones pointing down and backwards.

**ornithopods**
A group of plant-eating dinosaurs that normally walked on two legs.

**palaeontologist**
A scientist who studies fossils and life in ancient times.

**pelvis**
A group of bones where the legs join the back-bone.

**predator**
An animal that hunts and kills other animals to eat.

**reptile**
A scaly animal that lays shelled eggs, such as the turtles, snakes, lizards, and crocodiles of today. Dinosaurs were reptiles.

**saurischian dinosaur**
The lizard-hipped type of dinosaur with one of the two lower hip bones pointing down and forwards and the other bone pointing down and backwards.

**sauropod**
A group of large, plant-eating, lizard-hipped dinosaurs, one of which was *Barosaurus*.

**scavenger**
A meat-eater that feeds on prey that is already dead, rather than on prey that it has killed.

**skeleton**
The supporting bony frame inside an animal's body.

**specimen**
Something that is collected or preserved as an example from a particular group.

# PRONUNCIATION GUIDE

The following is a guide to pronunciation of the dinosaur names mentioned in this book.

**theropods**
All meat-eating lizard-hipped dinosaurs, such as *Tyrannosaurus rex*.

**Triassic Period**
Part of the Earth's history, which lasted from 248 to 205 million years ago, during which the dinosaurs first appeared.

**type specimen**
The one specimen of an animal or plant that is used as a standard to compare with other specimens.

**tyrannosaur**
Best-known family within the carnosaurs.

**vertebrae**
Bones that form the back-bone of animals.

**weathering**
When rocks and soil are broken up and washed or blown away by wind, rain, sun, frost, and other features of the weather.

- *Albertosaurus*
  (al-bert-oh-saw-rus)
- *Allosaurus*
  (al-low-saw-rus)
- *Ankylosaurus*
  (ank-kye-low-saw-rus)
- *Apatosaurus*
  (ap-pat-oh-saw-rus)

- *Barosaurus*
  (barrow-saw-rus)
- *Brachiosaurus*
  (brakky-oh-saw-rus)

- *Camarasaurus*
  (kam-ah-ra-saw-rus)
- *Camptosaurus*
  (camp-toe-saw-rus)
- *Centrosaurus*
  (sen-tro-saw-rus)
- *Ceratosaurus*
  (seratto-saw-rus)
- *Cetiosaurus*
  (seaty-oh-saw-rus)
- *Chasmosaurus*
  (kas-mo-saw-rus)
- *Corythosaurus*
  (korrith-oh-saw-rus)

- *Daspletosaurus*
  (dass-pleet-oh-saw-rus)
- *Deinonychus*
  (die-non-e-cus)
- *Dilophosaurus*
  (dye-loff-oh-saw-rus)
- *Diplodocus*
  (di-plod-ock-us)
- *Dryosaurus*
  (dry-oh-saw-rus)

- *Edmontosaurus*
  (ed-mon-toe-saw-rus)
- *Euoplocephalus*
  (you-oh-plo-keff-allus)

- *Hadrosaurus*
  (had-row-saw-rus)
- *Heterodontosaurus*
  (het-ter-row-dont-oh-saw-rus)
- *Hypacrosaurus*
  (hi-pack-row-saw-rus)

- *Iguanodon*
  (ig-wan-oh-don)

- *Kritosaurus*
  (krit-oh-saw-rus)

- *Lambeosaurus*
  (lam-bay-oh-saw-rus)

- *Maiasaura*
  (my-ah-saw-rah)
- *Mamenchisaurus*
  (mammenkey-saw-rus)
- *Monoclonius*
  (mon-oh-clone-e-us)
- *Montanoceratops*
  (mon-tan-oh-sera-tops)

- *Ornithomimus*
  (ornith-oh-meem-us)

- *Oviraptor*
  (ovi-rap-tor)

- *Pachycephalosaurus*
  (pakky-seph-ah-low-saw-rus)
- *Parasaurolophus*
  (para-saw-rol-oh-fus)
- *Pentaceratops*
  (pen-tah-ser-ah-tops)
- *Plateosaurus*
  (plat-ay-oh-saw-rus)
- *Prosaurolophus*
  (pro-saw-rol-oh-fus)
- *Protoceratops*
  (pro-toe-sera-tops)

- *Saurolophus*
  (saw-rol-oh-fus)
- *Stegosaurus*
  (stegg-oh-saw-rus)
- *Struthiomimus*
  (strewth-ee-yo-meem-us)
- *Styracosaurus*
  (sty-rack-oh-saw-rus)

- *Tarbosaurus*
  (tar-bow-saw-rus)
- *Torosaurus*
  (toe-row-saw-rus)
- *Triceratops*
  (try-ser-rah-tops)
- *Troodon*
  (tru-oh-don)
- *Tyrannosaurus rex*
  (tie-ran-oh-saw-rus recks)

# INDEX

# ACKNOWLEDGMENTS

Picture credits:
t=top, b=bottom, m=middle,
l=left, r=right

## TYRANNOSAURUS REX

Courtesy Department of Library Services, American Museum of Natural History: Neg. no. 37243, 9tr; Neg. no. 335782, 9mr; Neg. no. 18338, 10tl; Neg. no. 18341, 10mr; Neg. no. 121779, 10b; Neg. no. 35923, 11tr.

Model photography by Dave King 1bl, 1mr, 4br, 5, 12ml, 15t, 15br, 16, 17, 19-23.

Museum photography by Lynton Gardiner 11br, 12r, 13, 14br, 15tr, 18ml, 18, 19m, 24mr.

Additional special photography by Paul Bricknell (magnifying glass) 9tl; Andy Crawford 2t, 13bl, 24b; John Down 14r; Philip Dowell (ostrich leg bone); Tim Ridley 10tr; Harry Taylor 8bl; Jerry Young 6tr, 15tl.

## BAROSAURUS

Courtesy Department of Library Services, American Museum of Natural History: Neg. no. 37243, 33mr; The Carnegie Museum of Natural History: Neg. no. 1012, 31br; Special Collections, University of Utah Library: Neg. no. 860, 30bml; Neg. no. 815, 32tl; Neg. no. 763, 32m (upper); Neg. no. 798, 32m (lower); Neg. no. 815, 32bm; Neg. no. 1039, 32br.

Model photography by Dave King 1mr, 2br, 40bl, 42–45, 93br.

Museum photography by Lynton Gardiner 28bl, 28tr, 28mr, 31tl, 32bl, 32tr, 32mr, 33bl, 34–41, 46mr.

Additional special photography by Paul Bricknell (magnifying glass) 31br; Andy Crawford (children) 40, 41, 47; Colin Keates 44mr; Mary Ann Lynch 36tr; Tim Ridley 4tl, 34t, 34mr, 35tl, 46b, 47b.

Barosaurus scale model, 40tr, courtesy of Eugene Gaffney; designed by Shinobu Matsumura; manufactured by Kaiyodo Company Ltd, Japan.

## CORYTHOSAURUS

Courtesy Department of Library Services, American Museum of Natural History: Neg. no. 37243, 53tl; Neg. no. 18502, 53ml; Neg. no. 18547, 54m; Neg. no. 18552, 54br, 55bl; Neg. no. 19488, 55tr; Neg. no. 19493, 55mr; Sternberg files, M. Walker Collection, University Archives/ Forsyth Library; Fort Hays State University, Hays, Kansas: 54ml, 55tl; Bruce Coleman/Mark N. Boulton: 63mr. Bridgeman Art Library: 63br.

Model photography by Dave King: 1br, 1bm, 3tl, 4br, 48-51, 58, 59, 61b, 64–67, 68b, 71br, 93tl.

Museum photography by Lynton Gardiner: 52bl, 55br, 56–57, 60b, 62tr, 63tl, 65bl, 65br, 68mr.

Additional special photography by Paul Bricknell (magnifying glass): 53tr; Andy Crawford: (children) 56tr, 56bl, 57tr, 57br, 68b.

## TRICERATOPS

Courtesy Department of Library Services, American Museum of Natural History: Neg. no. 18541, 74b; Neg. no. 18375, 76tl; Neg. no. 253875, 84tr; Neg. no. 251518, 84ml; Neg. no. 411955, 84bl; Neg. no. 410764, 84br; AMNH/Fred Conrad: 84; Sternberg files, M. Walker Collection, University Archives/ Forsyth Library, Fort Hays State University, Hays, Kansas: 76ml, 76br, 77tl, 77ml, 77mr, 77br; permission of the National Museum of Canada, Ottawa: 76mr; Bruce Coleman/RIM Campbell: 83br.

Model photography by Dave King: 1tr, 1m, 3bm, 4tr, 70, 71tl, 71bl, 72b, 73bl, 78-79m, 79tm, 80-81, 82–83, 90b, 95b.

Museum photography by Lynton Gardiner: 75tl, 78–79b, 79tr, 86-87t, 87bl, 87r, 88-89, 90mr.

Additional special photography by Paul Bricknell: (magnifying glass) 75tr, 84mr; Andy Crawford: (children) 78bl, 90b, (model) 71r, 82tr; Jerry Young: 87m.

Dorling Kindersley would like to thank Katherine Rogers for her help in researching images from the Sternberg files at the Forsyth Library, Fort Hays State University, Hays, Kansas. Roger Priddy for art directing photography at the American Museum of Natural History, and Rowena Alsey, Jonathan Buckley, Mandy Earey, and Sharon Peters for their help in producing this book.

Jacket: model photography by Dave King.

Thanks also to Andrew Abello, Darren Chin, Natalie Ebrey, Jennie Joannides, Katy King, Daniel Ray, and Jamie Ross for appearing in this book.

Index by Lynn Bresler.